Grades 3–6

Operations Handbook

An Everyday Mathematics® Supplement

SRA

A Division of The McGraw·Hill Companies

Columbus, Ohio
Chicago, Illinois

www.sra4kids.com

SRA/McGraw-Hill

A Division of The **McGraw·Hill** *Companies*

Copyright © 2002 by SRA/McGraw-Hill.

Photo Credits
Cover: Bill Burlingham / Photography
Photo Collage: Herman Adler Design

Send all inquiries to:
SRA/McGraw-Hill
P.O. Box 812960
Chicago, IL 60681

Printed in the United States of America.

ISBN 1-57039-046-0

5 6 7 8 9 10 VHC 09 08 07 06 05 04

Contents

Introduction

Some people think of an algorithm *only as one of the step-by-step operational procedures students learn in school mathematics. Actually, an algorithm is any reliable procedure or routine that, when followed properly, leads to a specific, expected, and guaranteed outcome. Furthermore, most people use many different algorithms every day:*

- *Operating a microwave oven*
- *Programming a VCR*
- *Playing a computer game*
- *Balancing a checkbook*

Each of the algorithms involved in such everyday activities is, of course, in part a mathematics application. Teaching students to become comfortable with algorithmic and procedural thinking is essential to their growth and development as everyday problem solvers.

Teaching Algorithmic Thinking

Algorithms are often taught in the following manner: First, young children explore and experiment with concrete models of numbers and operations. Then, students gradually move beyond concrete representations to pictorial representations. At these two stages, number symbols (numerals) are used along with their concrete or pictorial counterparts. Finally, students are ready to work with symbols only.

Such a progression—from the concrete to the pictorial to the symbolic—builds students' understanding of numeration, basic facts, and operations and culminates in students learning standard paper-and-pencil algorithms for addition, subtraction, multiplication, and division of whole numbers, decimals, and fractions.

While the teaching of a single standard paper-and-pencil algorithm per operation is still seen by many educators and mathematicians as an important part of elementary mathematics instruction, there is an increasing emphasis on including alternative algorithms as well.

One problem with offering students only one algorithm per operation is that they tend to "over-apply" the algorithm. For example, even when a quick mental-math procedure suffices and, indeed, is preferable (as is the case with a problem as simple as 400 – 2), many students tend to resort to the paper-and-pencil algorithm. Furthermore, students often "learn" the algorithm with little understanding of it and sometimes assume that their answers are correct simply because they have performed the prescribed procedures!

Conversely, students who are developing sound *number sense* do not automatically categorize a given problem, such as 400 – 2, as an addition or subtraction problem. Instead, students *analyze* each problem and then use whichever operation is most efficient or convenient to solve it. Such students are reflective and creative in their use of the four operations, and they do not blindly use ready-made algorithms as substitutes for thinking and common sense.

Developing Number Sense

People with good number sense:

- are flexible in their thinking about numbers and arithmetic and look for "shortcuts" to make their efforts more efficient;

- are continually cultivating good mental-math skills, along with reliable algorithms and procedures for finding results they can't produce mentally;

- can use their number and arithmetic skills to solve problems in everyday situations; and

- can recognize unreasonable results when they see numbers in print, in other media—or in their own work.

Because *Everyday Mathematics* views computational algorithms as much more than rote processes, the program aims to make students active participants in the analysis of various alternative algorithms—and in the development of new ones.

One of the best ways to encourage students to participate in such activities is for the teacher to model his or her own thinking processes for the class. When working through an example on the board, for instance, the teacher should not hesitate to verbalize every thought—especially those that express doubt, questions, and trial and error. Students greatly benefit from—and are inspired by—recognizing that mathematics is not just a collection of procedures to be memorized, but a way of thinking to be tried, adapted, and modified to suit one's own needs. It is important for students to see their teacher question his or her own methods—and then try a different method if necessary.

Encouraging Algorithm Development

It is helpful to remember that every algorithm was, at the time of its invention, developed in response to a perceived need for greater speed, greater accuracy, greater convenience, or clearer instruction.

When students create—and share—their own problem-solving methodologies instead of simply learning a prescribed (and limited) set of standard algorithms, they become active and enthusiastic participants in their learning process. They begin to realize that any problem can be solved in more than one way. Students become motivated and independent problem solvers who are able to take risks, think logically, and reason analytically. They improve their understanding of place value and sharpen their estimation and mental-computation skills.

In order to create an environment in which students can create new algorithms and adapt existing ones to meet their own needs and learning styles, teachers must allow students adequate time to explore with concrete materials, develop mental-math strategies, and experiment using paper and pencil.

Focus Algorithms

Everday Mathematics also includes a "focus" algorithm for each operation with whole numbers and decimals. Focus algorithms are powerful, relatively efficient, and easy to understand and learn. At some point, all students should master the focus algorithm for each operation. In solving problems, however, students may use either the focus algorithm or any other methods they choose. The aim of this approach is to promote flexibility while ensuring that all students know at least one reliable method for each operation. There are two additional pages of problems for each focus algorithm.

On the next page are some suggestions for helping students invent new algorithms, as well as analyze and adapt existing algorithms.

Allow time for students to explore problems using physical models and/or paper and pencil.

- Present a problem.
- Have groups work on the problem.
- Encourage students to use base-10 blocks, arrays, and other materials to explore and model their thinking.
- Have groups share their strategies and solutions with the rest of the class.

Provide problems in contexts that have appropriate grade-level applications.

- Choose problems that are meaningful to students.
- Encourage students to find and create their own problems.

Help children build basic-facts knowledge and strategies.

- Use doubles.
- Use doubles-plus-one.
- Use +0, +1, and −1.
- Use skip counting.
- Use sums of ten.
- Use easier numbers.
- Use counting up.
- Use all available shortcuts.

Include collaborative learning whenever possible.

- Encourage students to share their thinking within their groups.
- Model think-aloud strategies for students.
- Have students record their solution methods.
- Have students share various problem-solving strategies with the rest of the class.

Alternative and invented algorithms can also be efficient means for working with geometry, as well as averaging and estimating. For more information on these and other uses of traditional and nontraditional algorithms, see Section 3.5, "Algorithmic and Procedural Thinking" of the Algorithms essay, in the *Teacher's Reference Manual*.

Everyday Mathematics encourages you to observe your students' algorithmic and procedural thinking when they are engaged in activities dealing with topics other than computation. For example, one student may have an algorithmic approach to drawing geometric figures or patterns, and another may invent ways to convert metric measures by "moving" decimal points. Have students share their algorithms with the class. Algorithms might even be named after their inventors and entered into an algorithm database.

Everyday Mathematics aims to provide all students with dependable and understandable methods for computation. The program recognizes that computation is an important and practical part of mathematics and has been designed to ensure that all students can compute accurately in a variety of ways.

Using the *Operations Handbook*

The *Operations Handbook* may be used as a supplement to the *Everyday Mathematics* program. The handbook outlines several of the many possible algorithms for each operation and is based on the *Everyday Mathematics* belief that because children begin their school years with intuitive mathematics skills, they are quite capable of adapting both traditional and nontraditional algorithms to suit their individual strengths and purposes.

The handbook contains most of the algorithms used and discussed in the *Everyday Mathematics* materials and a few additional ones as well.

For each algorithm, there is a **teaching notes page** on the left and a **student page** on the right. The **student page** can be made into an instructional transparency or duplicated for each child.

Look for the following features on each teaching notes page:
  • a brief description of the algorithm
  • an activity designed to help build understanding of the algorithm
  • questioning strategies to help you guide your students through the examples
  • an "Error Alert" and techniques for dealing with common errors
  • suggestions for checking student understanding
  • answers to the "Check Your Understanding" exercises on the facing student page

Look for the following features on each student page:
  • step-by-step directions for following the algorithm
  • one or two examples
  • "Check Your Understanding" exercises, with problems presented in order of difficulty and culminating in a challenge problem, identified by an asterisk

Practice Sets

At the back of this handbook (pages 86 – 165) there are twenty paired sets of mixed computation practice. There are five paired sets for each grade.

Grade 3   Practice Sets 1A/B, 2A/B, 3A/B, 4A/B, 5A/B
Grade 4   Practice Sets 6A/B, 7A/B, 8A/B, 9A/B, 10A/B
Grade 5   Practice Sets 11A/B, 12A/B, 13A/B, 14A/B, 15A/B
Grade 6   Practice Sets 16A/B, 17A/B, 18A/B, 19A/B, 20A/B

The A/B pairings contain the same type and level of practice. For example, Practice Sets 16A/B both emphasize addition, subtraction, multiplication, and division of whole numbers and decimals. The types of computation and numerals emphasized on each paired set are indicated on the teacher answer pages. Naturally, more skilled third graders might benefit from higher-level practice, while less skilled sixth graders might benefit from lower-level practice. Note that the grade level suggestion for each set is only indicated on the teacher answer page to allow for maximum flexibility and use of student Practice Sets.

Note that both horizontal and vertical formats are used for the problems on these Practice Set pages and that *Everyday Mathematics* uses two symbols for multiplication ($\times$ and $*$) and three symbols for division (/ and $\div$ and $\overline{)}$). Additionally, *Everyday Mathematics* uses an arrow $\longrightarrow$ for division problems that result in quotients with remainders because, for example, "$64 \div 7 = 9$ R1" is not a true number sentence.

Partial-Sums Algorithm for Addition

The partial-sums algorithm for addition is particularly useful for adding multidigit numbers. As the name suggests, a person using this algorithm first calculates partial sums, working one place-value column at a time, and then adds all the partial sums to find the total sum.

The partial sums are easier numbers to work with, and students feel empowered when they discover that, with practice, they can use this algorithm to add numbers mentally.

Build Understanding

Tell students that one way to add larger numbers is to add them one place-value column at a time. Write the number 3,714 on the board. Have a volunteer come to the board and separate the place-value columns in the number by drawing lines between the digits. Then direct another student to write letter abbreviations (Th, H, T, and O) above the digits to show the value of each place.

Using page 9, explain that with this method of adding, the numbers will be added one place-value at a time. Although the columns can be added in any order, working from left to right—that is, from the greatest place value to the least—is the usual procedure. Use questions like the following to guide students through the examples:

- What is the greatest place value in the top (or the greater) addend?

- What is the second-greatest place value in that addend?

- Does each addend have a digit in the (hundreds) place?

- Where is the plus sign written for the partial sums? *(next to the last partial sum)*

Explain the addition in Example 1 in this way: 8 hundreds plus 2 hundreds are 10 hundreds; 800 plus 200 is 1,000 (and so on). Modeling this kind of place-value language for students while working through the examples—and encouraging students to use this language as well—help emphasize the fact that students are adding partial sums before finding the total sum.

Error Alert In Example 1, if students seem confused about which number is the total of 835 and 243, review the meaning of the word "partial." Make sure students understand that each number written between the lines represents a part of the final sum. The final sum or total is written below the second line.

Check Understanding

Write 719 + 503 on the board. Have two volunteers demonstrate the computation for this problem using the partial-sums algorithm. Invite one student to write and the other to narrate. Use additional examples if necessary. When you are reasonably certain that most of your students understand the algorithm, assign the "Check Your Understanding" exercises at the bottom of page 9. For practice of more difficult problems, refer students to pages 10–11. *(See answers in margin.)*

Partial-Sums Algorithm for Addition

Add one place-value column at a time.
Write each partial sum below the problem.
Then add all the partial sums to find the total sum.

Example 1

$$\begin{array}{r} 835 \\ +\ 243 \\ \hline \end{array}$$

Add the hundreds.	→	*(800 + 200)*	→ 1,000
Add the tens.	→	*(30 + 40)*	→ 70
Add the ones.	→	*(5 + 3)*	→ + 8
Add the partial sums.	→	*(1,000 + 70 + 8)*	→ **1,078**

Example 2

$$\begin{array}{r} 945 \\ +\ 468 \\ \hline \end{array}$$

Add the hundreds.	→	*(900 + 400)*	→ 1,300
Add the tens.	→	*(40 + 60)*	→ 100
Add the ones.	→	*(5 + 8)*	→ + 13
Add the partial sums.	→	*(1,300 + 100 + 13)*	→ **1,413**

Check Your Understanding

Solve the following problems:

1. 405 + 377 **2.** 811 + 463 **3.** 931 + 850

4. 809 + 299 **5.** 912 + 756 **6.** 257 + 789

7. 3,098 + 234 **8.** 4,078 + 706

Write your answers on a separate sheet of paper. **Addition Algorithms 9**

Partial-Sums Algorithm for Addition

Add one place-value column at a time.
Write each partial sum below the problem.
Then add all the partial sums to find the total sum.

Example 1

$$\begin{array}{r} 6,089 \\ +\ 7,925 \end{array}$$

Add the thousands.	→	(6,000 + 7,000)	→ 13,000
Add the hundreds.	→	(0 + 900)	→ 900
Add the tens.	→	(80 + 20)	→ 100
Add the ones.	→	(9 + 5)	→ + 14
Add the partial sums.	→	(13,000 + 900 + 100 + 14)	→ **14,014**

Example 2

$$\begin{array}{r} 9,838 \\ +\ 7,399 \end{array}$$

Add the thousands.	→	(9,000 + 7,000)	→ 16,000
Add the hundreds.	→	(800 + 300)	→ 1,100
Add the tens.	→	(30 + 90)	→ 120
Add the ones.	→	(8 + 9)	→ + 17
Add the partial sums.	→	(16,000 + 1,100 + 120 + 17)	→ **17,237**

Check Your Understanding

Solve the following problems:

1. 4,397 + 1,158   **2.** 3,066 + 2,583   **3.** 5,932 + 4,059

4. 8,675 + 3,009   **5.** 4,598 + 2,094   **6.** 9,362 + 6,256

7. 23,409 + 2,967   **8.** 9,458 + 5,371 + 6,798

Write your answers on a separate sheet of paper.

Partial-Sums Algorithm for Addition

Add one place-value column at a time.
Write each partial sum below the problem.
Then add all the partial sums to find the total sum.

Example 1

$$\begin{array}{r} 23{,}609 \\ +\ 45{,}984 \end{array}$$

Add the ten-thousands. →	(20,000 + 40,000)	→	60,000
Add the thousands. →	(3,000 + 5,000)	→	8,000
Add the hundreds. →	(600 + 900)	→	1,500
Add the tens. →	(0 + 80)	→	80
Add the ones. →	(9 + 4)	→ +	13
Add the partial sums. →	(60,000 + 8,000 + 1,500 + 80 + 13) →		**69,593**

Example 2

$$\begin{array}{r} 45{,}987 \\ +\ 94{,}421 \end{array}$$

Add the ten-thousands. →	(40,000 + 90,000)	→	130,000
Add the thousands. →	(5,000 + 4,000)	→	9,000
Add the hundreds. →	(900 + 400)	→	1,300
Add the tens. →	(80 + 20)	→	100
Add the ones. →	(7 + 1)	→ +	8
Add the partial sums. →	(130,000 + 9,000 + 1,300 + 100 + 8) →		**140,408**

Check Your Understanding

Solve the following problems:

1. 45,896 + 12,509   **2.** 56,982 + 23,445   **3.** 98,456 + 67,382

4. 65,076 + 18,691   **5.** 74,375 + 42,009   **6.** 29,855 + 87,633

7. 34,429 + 305,782   **8.** 19,568 + 39,537 + 87,068

Column-Addition Algorithm for Addition

The column-addition algorithm for addition allows people to work with the place-value columns in any order. It also allows them to write both digits of each partial answer directly underneath the appropriate column and then, if necessary, to go back and adjust the partial answers to find the final answer.

Many students find this algorithm very natural—and instructive.

Build Understanding

Using page 13, explain that with this method of adding, students will add the digits in each column in any order, write individual place-value answers as they go, and then, if necessary, go back and adjust those partial answers to find the final answer. Use questions like the following to guide students through the examples:

- Which two numbers will you begin with? *(It doesn't matter. The columns can be added in any order.)*

- Where do you write the sum for each column? *(In the same column directly beneath the digits being added.)*

- How do you adjust the place-value answers? *(If the sum in a column has two digits, write down the ones digit and add a 1 to the answer in the column to the left.)*

While working through Example 1, model appropriate place-value language: "2 hundreds plus 4 hundreds are 6 hundreds; 6 tens plus 8 tens are 14 tens; and 8 ones plus 3 ones are 11 ones. ... Now, we have 14 tens and since 10 tens equal 1 hundred, we have 7 hundreds and 4 tens. ... We have 11 ones and since 10 ones equal 1 ten, we have 5 tens and 1 one." (When working through Example 2, point out that another name for "14 hundreds" is "1 thousand, 4 hundreds.")

Error Alert To help students organize both their thinking and their writing, encourage them to put extra space between the digits in each addend and to draw vertical lines to separate the place-value columns.

Check Understanding

Make sure students understand that the final sum in Example 1 is 751. If necessary, work through additional examples on the board. When you are reasonably certain that most of your students understand the algorithm, assign the "Check Your Understanding" exercises at the bottom of page 13. *(See answers in margin.)*

Page 13
Answer Key

1. 1,275

2. 821

3. 582

4. 913

5. 1,082

6. 1,152

7. 2,626

8. 8,348

Column-Addition Algorithm for Addition

Add one place-value column at a time. Write each place-value answer directly beneath the problem. Then go back and adjust each place-value answer, if necessary, one column at a time.

Example 1

$$
\begin{array}{r}
2\ \ 6\ \ 8 \\
+\ 4\ \ 8\ \ 3 \\
\hline
\end{array}
$$

Add the digits in each column.	→	6	14	11
If necessary, adjust the hundreds and the tens.	→	7	4	11
If necessary, adjust the tens and the ones.	→	**7**	**5**	**1**

Example 2

$$
\begin{array}{r}
9\ \ 6\ \ 7 \\
+\ 4\ \ 9\ \ 5 \\
\hline
\end{array}
$$

Add the digits in each column.	→	13	15	12
If necessary, adjust the hundreds and the tens.	→	14	5	12
If necessary, adjust the tens and the ones.	→	**1,4**	**6**	**2**

Check Your Understanding

Solve the following problems:

1. 511 + 764

2. 703 + 118

3. 303 + 279

4. 442 + 471

5. 453 + 629

6. 862 + 290

7. 1,859 + 767

8. 1,095 + 2,817 + 4,436

Opposite-Change Rule for Addition

The opposite-change rule says that if a number is added to one addend and that same number is subtracted from the other addend, the sum will be unaffected. And since it is arguably easier to add two addends when one of them ends in one or more zeros, the goal is to adjust both addends so that one of them is changed to the nearest ten (or hundred or thousand).

Students find this algorithm particularly useful when calculating mentally.

Build Understanding

Lead students in a quick, oral review of number pairs that add up to 10. Then expand the review by asking students to identify number pairs that add up to 20, 30, 40, 50, and so on. Point out to students that these larger multiples-of-ten number pairs are based on basic addition facts—for example, the 42 and 8 pair is based on 2 and 8; the 31 and 9 pair is based on 1 and 9; and the 25 and 5 pair is based on 5 and 5. Then reverse the review and test students on multiples-of-ten number pairs based on basic subtraction facts: *What is 40 minus 3? 70 minus 6? 90 minus 8?*

Note: Some students may need to write the basic facts and fact extensions on scratch paper. Others may need to see a demonstration: Display 10 counters and have different students demonstrate how many different subgroup pairings can be made with the ten counters while still maintaining the same total number (10).

Using page 15, explain that with this method of adding, students will be renaming the two addends (and rewriting the problem) one or two times before they finally add—the goal being to adjust both addends so that one of them ends in one or more zeros. Use questions like the following to guide students through the examples:

- Which of the two addends is closer to an even ten (or hundred or thousand)?
- How much will you have to add to (or subtract from) that addend to make it an even ten (or hundred or thousand)?
- What will you have to do to the other addend?
- Do you need to adjust the addends again before you are ready to add them together?

Error Alert Watch for students who adjust one addend "up" or "down" without also adjusting the other addend the opposite way. Explain that students are taking the total value of the two numbers and shifting it around, or redistributing it, between the two addends. To maintain the total value, they cannot add a number to one addend without subtracting that same number from the other addend.

Check Understanding

Divide the class into groups of four, and assign a leader in each group to explain which adjustments took place in each of the examples. Tell group members to direct their questions to their group's leader. When you are reasonably certain that most of your students understand the algorithm, assign the "Check Your Understanding" exercises at the bottom of page 15. *(See answers in margin.)*

Page 15 Answer Key

1. 1,480
2. 912
3. 1,367
4. 4,227
5. 4,540
6. 2,113
7. 5,964
8. 20,600

Opposite-Change Rule for Addition

Decide which addend is closer to an even 10 (or 100 or 1,000).
Decide how to adjust that addend so that it ends in one or more zeros.
Adjust the other addend in the opposite way.
Rename both addends until you reach your goal.
Then add the two addends together to find their sum.

Example 1

$$364 \text{ (addend)}$$
$$+\ 278 \text{ (addend)}$$

First, adjust 364 down (by 2) to 362
and adjust 278 up (by 2) to 280.

$$362$$
$$+\ 280$$

Then, adjust 362 down (by 20) to 342
and adjust 280 up (by 20) to 300.
Finally, add the two addends together. →

$$342$$
$$+\ 300$$
$$\mathbf{642} \text{ (sum)}$$

Example 2

$$5,261$$
$$+9,400$$

First, adjust 9,400 down (by 400) to 9,000
and adjust 5,261 up (by 400) to 5,661.
Then add the two addends together. →

$$5,661$$
$$+\ 9,000$$
$$\mathbf{14,661}$$

Check Your Understanding

Solve the following problems:

1. 504 + 976   **2.** 642 + 270   **3.** 823 + 544

4. 4,132 + 95   **5.** 972 + 3,568   **6.** 1,477 + 636

7. 2,675 + 3,289   **8.** 14,037 + 6,563

Write your answers on a separate sheet of paper.

Short Algorithm (Standard) for Addition (with Models)

The short algorithm (standard) for addition is the one that is familiar to most adults and many children. A person using this algorithm adds from right to left, one place-value column at a time, regrouping as necessary.

The traditional method for teaching this algorithm is to begin with concrete models (such as base-10 blocks), using them to demonstrate the regrouping process.

Build Understanding

Divide the class into small groups, pass out place-value blocks to each group, and have each group model the number 117. When all groups have set up their models correctly, tell them to add 6 to the number they have built. If necessary, remind students to regroup the 7 original ones and the 6 new ones into ones and tens. Check each group's final model.

Using page 17, explain that with this method of adding, students will begin on the right with the ones and then move one place-value column at a time to the left. Use questions like the following to guide students through the example:

- What do you have to do when you add 6 ones and 9 ones? (*Trade 10 ones for 1 ten.*)

- What do you have to do when you add 1 ten and 1 ten and 9 tens? (*Trade 10 tens for 1 hundred.*)

- In the diagram or model that represents the sum, what has changed from the two models above it? (*The blocks from the two previous models have been combined to show the regrouping, or the trading, that has taken place.*)

Error Alert Watch for students who do not align addends and sums correctly, because misalignment can lead to incorrect regrouping and wrong answers. Encourage students to allow themselves plenty of room to write the problems out. If necessary, tell students to put a pencil width of space between each digit, or have students write the problems on grid paper.

Check Understanding

Write 329 + 584 on the board. Have a volunteer explain how to solve the problem. Question the student's choices if necessary, but do not write anything on the board unless the student directs you to. Allow the volunteer to solicit help if necessary. When you are reasonably certain that most of your students understand the algorithm, assign the "Check Your Understanding" exercises at the bottom of page 17. (*See answers in margin.*)

Short Algorithm (Standard) for Addition (with Models)

Use blocks to model the problem. Add from right to left.
Then find the total.

Example

	HUNDREDS	TENS	ONES	
				$\begin{array}{r} 216 \\ + 199 \\ \hline \end{array}$
Add the ones. Trade 10 ones for 1 ten.				$\begin{array}{r} \overset{1}{2}16 \\ + 199 \\ \hline 5 \end{array}$
Add the tens. Trade 10 tens for 1 hundred.				$\begin{array}{r} \overset{1\,1}{2}16 \\ + 199 \\ \hline 15 \end{array}$
Add the hundreds. **415** is the total.				$\begin{array}{r} \overset{1\,1}{2}16 \\ + 199 \\ \hline 415 \end{array}$

Check Your Understanding

Solve the following problems:

1. 341 + 76   **2.** 509 + 367   **3.** 92 + 811

4. 733 + 587   **5.** 936 + 88   **6.** 269 + 185

7. 3,968 + 4,075   **8.** 4,172 + 1,693 + 1,568

Write your answers on a separate sheet of paper.

Short Algorithm (Standard) for Addition

The short algorithm (standard) for addition is the one that is familiar to most adults and many children. A person using this algorithm adds from right to left, one place-value column at a time, regrouping as necessary.

The traditional method for teaching this algorithm is to begin with concrete models (such as base-10 blocks) and then gradually move toward the use of symbols (that is, numerals) only.

Build Understanding

Tell students to count to 54 in unison with you on their fingers. Begin counting. When you arrive at 11, ask students how they think they might keep track of the tens. Guide students to see that they will need a mark of some kind—a check mark on the board, for example—for each set of ten. (You might wish to have students record their own symbols on paper at their desks while you record those same symbols on the board.) Place one check mark on the board to help everyone remember that you have 1 ten already. Then continue counting. At 21, ask the class what to do. Guide students to continue using the agreed-upon symbol to keep track of the tens. At 54, ask students how they might adjust the notation to record the fact that they do not have another set of ten; they have only a set of four. Guide students to complete their symbolic notation with tally marks (or some other kind of marks) to stand for the 4 ones. Then have the class count and read its "number" (✔✔✔✔✔////) in unison.

Using page 19, explain that with this method of adding, students will begin on the right with the ones and then move one place-value column at a time to the left. Use questions like the following to guide students through the example (and through other examples you provide):

- Which two numbers will you add first? *(the ones)*
- How will you show an extra ten? *(Record a 1 over the tens place.)*
- What do you have to remember when adding a column of numbers? *(to add the regrouped number, if there is one, along with the other numbers in that column)*

Error Alert Watch for students who write the regrouped ten (or hundred or thousand) over the wrong place-value column. Some students may benefit from drawing vertical lines between the columns so that they can track where to write the regrouped digits. Other students may be able to do the regrouping mentally and not need to record visual "reminders."

Check Understanding

Have a student make up a problem that he or she considers easy and write it on the board. Then ask a volunteer to come to the board, solve the problem, and explain the solution process. Work through as many problems as you feel are necessary, until you are reasonably certain that most of your students understand the algorithm. Then assign the "Check Your Understanding" exercises at the bottom of page 19. *(See answers in margin.)*

Page 19 Answer Key

1. 601
2. 938
3. 955
4. 523
5. 811
6. 8,658
7. 4,620
8. 16,275

Short Algorithm (Standard) for Addition

Begin adding on the right, and then move to the left. Regroup each partial answer, if necessary, by writing each digit in the appropriate place-value column.

Example

$$\begin{array}{r} 588 \\ +\ 143 \end{array}$$

Add the ones. *(8 ones + 3 ones = 11 ones)*
Regroup. *(11 ones = 1 ten and 1 one)* $\longrightarrow$

$$\begin{array}{r} {\scriptstyle 1} \\ 588 \\ +\ 143 \\ \hline 1 \end{array}$$

Add the tens. *(1 ten + 8 tens + 4 tens = 13 tens)* $\longrightarrow$
Regroup. *(13 tens = 1 hundred and 3 tens)*

$$\begin{array}{r} {\scriptstyle 1\ 1} \\ 588 \\ +\ 143 \\ \hline 31 \end{array}$$

Add the hundreds. *(1 hundred + 5 hundreds + 1 hundred = 7 hundreds)* $\longrightarrow$

731 is the total.

$$\begin{array}{r} {\scriptstyle 1} \\ 588 \\ +\ 143 \\ \hline 731 \end{array}$$

Check Your Understanding

Solve the following problems:

1. 582 + 19

2. 748 + 190

3. 856 + 99

4. 307 + 216

5. 236 + 575

6. 8,163 + 495

7. 2,641 + 1,979

8. 5,219 + 3,487 + 7,569

Write your answers on a separate sheet of paper.

Partial-Sums Algorithm for Decimal Addition

Just as they do with whole numbers, problem solvers add decimals by adding values of digits one place–value column at a time—whether tens or tenths, hundreds or hundredths, and so on. The partial-sums algorithm and the column-addition algorithm used for adding multidigit whole numbers can easily be applied to decimal addition as long as the problem solver is careful to keep track of the place values—both whole-number and decimal place values.

Students will feel empowered as they discover that they can apply their number sense and understanding of whole-number addition to decimal situations. The key, as with whole-number addition, is to pay attention to the place values, and consequently the decimal point, in each of the addends.

Build Understanding

Discuss equivalent decimals like 7.3, 7.30, and 7.300. Then have students annex zeros to find equivalent decimals for 6.7, 0.4, 0.023, and 9. You may also want to review the whole-number versions of this algorithm on pages 8–11.

As you work through Example 1 on page 21, point out that the partial sums should be written with the same number of decimal places as the addend with the greater (or greatest) number of decimal places. Use questions like the following to guide students through the examples:

- Does it matter which place-value column you add first? *(No.)*

- In Example 1, why are 6 ones written as 6.000? *(to show the same number of decimal places as the addend with the greater number of decimal places. In this example, both 4.658 and 2.761 happen to have the same number of decimal places—three.)*

Error Alert Watch for students who do not write all the partial sums and the answer with the same number of decimal places. If students have difficulty with this, they may first need to review place value.

Check Understanding

Write 5.298 + 3.44 on the board. Have a volunteer work the problem using the partial-sums algorithm. Encourage the student to "narrate" his or her thought process. Encourage the class to ask questions, and guide the volunteer in answering as necessary. When you are reasonably certain that most of your students understand the algorithm, assign the "Check Your Understanding" exercises at the bottom of page 21. *(See answers in margin.)*

Page 21
Answer Key

1. 6.166

2. 67.84

3. 1.002

4. 0.034

5. 6.291

6. 18.029

7. 102.02

8. 5.914

Partial-Sums Algorithm for Decimal Addition

Use what you already know about adding whole numbers.
Add one place-value column at a time.
Remember to pay attention to the place values of the addends to record the decimal point in the sum.

Example 1

				4.658
				+ 2.761
Add the ones.	→	(4.000 + 2.000)	→	6.000
Add the tenths.	→	(0.600 + 0.700)	→	1.300
Add the hundredths.	→	(0.050 + 0.060)	→	0.110
Add the thousandths.	→	(0.008 + 0.001)	→	+ 0.009
Add the partial sums.	→	(6.000 + 1.300 + 0.110 + 0.009)	→	**7.419**

Example 2

				9.682
				+ 1.506
Add the ones.	→	(9.000 + 1.000)	→	10.000
Add the tenths.	→	(0.600 + 0.500)	→	1.100
Add the hundredths.	→	(0.080 + 0)	→	0.080
Add the thousandths.	→	(0.002 + 0.006)	→	+ 0.008
Add the partial sums.	→	(10.000 + 1.100 + 0.080 + 0.008)	→	**11.188**

Check Your Understanding

Solve the following problems:

1. 3.441 + 2.725

2. 60.45 + 7.39

3. 0.906 + 0.096

4. 0.006 + 0.028

5. 2.4 + 3.891

6. 12.34 + 5.689

7. 89.22 + 12.8

8. 5 + 0.034 + 0.88

Write your answers on a separate sheet of paper.

Short Algorithm (Standard) for Decimal Addition

The short algorithm (standard) for adding decimals is one that is familiar to most adults and many children. Those who are proficient in using the standard algorithm with whole numbers should be able to apply their knowledge and skills to decimal situations quite easily. The algorithm and the regrouping process are basically the same. Attention to place value is important because the problem solver always adds the values of digits one place-value column at a time—whether those digits are tens or tenths, hundreds or hundredths, and so on.

Build Understanding

If students need to review the whole-number version of this algorithm, refer them to page 19.

Using page 23, explain that with this method of adding decimals, students will begin by rewriting the problem so that the decimal points of both numbers are vertically aligned. If both addends do not have the same number of decimal places, students will rewrite one of the addends using zeros so that both numbers have the same number of decimal places. You may need to remind students that annexing zeros after the last digit to the right of a decimal point will not change a number's value. Use equivalent fractions, such as $\frac{1}{10} = \frac{10}{100} = \frac{100}{1,000}$, to show students that 0.1 = 0.10 = 0.100.

Students will then add as they would with the standard algorithm for adding whole numbers. Tell students to begin adding on the right and then move to the left one place-value column at a time. Remind students that when digits in a column add up to 10 or more, they will need to regroup. Use questions like the following to guide students through the examples:

- Why must you align the decimal points? *(so that you add ones to ones, tenths to tenths, and so on)*

- In Example 1, what does the 1 written above the 8 stand for? *(1 tenth)*

- In Example 2, why is 1.3 rewritten as 1.300? *(so that both addends will have the same number of decimal places)*

- Where do you put the decimal point in your answer? *(in the same place as the decimal points in the problem)*

Error Alert Watch for students who right-align the numbers, ignoring the position of the decimal point. Also, watch for students who do not include a decimal point in the answer. If it helps students, allow them to draw a vertical line to indicate the position of the decimal point. They write the decimal portion of the answer to the right of the line and the whole-number portion to the left. The line shows students the position of the decimal point in the answer.

Check Understanding

Divide students into pairs and have them solve the problem 4.9 + 3.28. Tell them to write neatly, and then have them exchange papers with their partners. Direct students to check each other's work. If they find a mistake, ask them to circle and identify the mistake. When you are reasonably certain that most of your students understand the algorithm, assign the "Check Your Understanding" exercises at the bottom of page 23. *(See answers in margin.)*

Page 23
Answer Key

1. 13.51

2. 1.72

3. 0.878

4. 2.089

5. 11.08

6. 10.689

7. 1.1758

8. 8.2251

Short Algorithm (Standard) for Decimal Addition

Align the addends in a column by place value.
Add from right to left as you would with whole numbers.
Regroup if necessary. Record the decimal point in the sum.

Example 1

$$9.84 + 3.39$$

a. Align the decimal points.
b. Add from right to left.
c. Regroup if necessary.
d. Place the decimal point in your answer.

$$
\begin{array}{r}
\overset{1\ 1}{9.84} \\
+\ 3.39 \\
\hline
13.23
\end{array}
$$

$$9.84 + 3.39 = 13.23$$

Example 2

$$0.734 + 1.3$$

a. Align the decimal points.
b. Rewrite 1.3 as 1.300.
c. Add from right to left.
d. Regroup as necessary.
e. Place the decimal point in your answer.

$$
\begin{array}{r}
\overset{1}{0.734} \\
+1.300 \\
\hline
2.034
\end{array}
$$

$$0.734 + 1.3 = 2.034$$

Check Your Understanding

Solve the following problems:

1. 8.32 + 5.19

2. 0.23 + 1.49

3. 0.386 + 0.492

4. 1.33 + 0.759

5. 4.98 + 6.1

6. 7 + 3.689

7. 0.53 + 0.6458

8. 3.8951 + 4.33

Write your answers on a separate sheet of paper.

Algorithms for Fraction Addition (with Models)

Fraction addition requires a firm understanding of the meaning of a fraction's numerator (the number of fractional parts at hand) and denominator (the number of fractional parts in the whole) as well as facility in naming equivalent fractions.

When adding two or more fractions with like denominators, the problem solver simply adds the numerators or the number of fractional parts in each addend. The denominator that shows the number of fractional parts in the whole does not change.

When adding fractions that have unlike denominators, the problem solver must first rename the addends using a common denominator.

Build Understanding

Review the process of finding common multiples. Have students list a few multiples of 4 *(4, 8, 12, 16, 20, 24)* and 6 *(6, 12, 18, 24, 30, 36)*. Then ask them to circle any numbers that are on both lists. Tell students that the circled numbers are common multiples of 4 and 6. If necessary, have students find common multiples of other number pairs, such as 4 and 10, 6 and 8, and 6 and 9.

Using page 25, explain that when adding fractions with different denominators, students will need to find a common multiple of the denominators, or a common denominator. Then, they will rename these fractions using this common denominator. You may want to explain that renaming fractions will be easier if students use the smallest common denominator. Use questions like the following to guide students through the examples:

- If you add fractions with the same denominator, what do you do to the numerators? *(You add them.)* What do you do to the denominator? *(Nothing. It stays the same.)*

- In Example 2, what is a common denominator of $\frac{1}{3}$ and $\frac{3}{4}$? *(12)*

- To rename $\frac{1}{3}$ with a denominator of 12, which number will you multiply each part of the fraction by? *(4, because 3 * 4 = 12)*

- To rename $\frac{3}{4}$ with a denominator of 12, which number will you multiply each part of the fraction by? *(3, because 4 * 3 = 12)*

Error Alert Watch for students who add denominators. If it helps these students, tell them to draw a diagram for each problem. This will help them see the denominator as the number of fractional parts in the *whole*. Also, watch for students who have difficulty finding common denominators. Explain to students that an easy way to find a common denominator of two fractions is to find the product of the two denominators.

Check Understanding

Divide the class into groups of 3 and ask each group to solve the problem $\frac{1}{2} + \frac{2}{5}$. Have one member of the group draw a diagram of the problem. Have the other members use the algorithm. The group members then compare their answers to make sure they are the same. If they are not the same, have the group members correct the error. When you are reasonably certain that most of your students understand the algorithm, assign the "Check Your Understanding" exercises at the bottom of page 25. *(See answers in margin.)*

***Page 25
Answer Key***

1. $\frac{6}{7}$

2. $\frac{3}{4}$

3. $1\frac{2}{3}$

4. $\frac{7}{12}$

5. $\frac{5}{8}$

6. $\frac{5}{6}$

7. $\frac{17}{24}$

8. $1\frac{1}{24}$

Algorithms for Fraction Addition (with Models)

Check that the addends have like denominators.
Then add the numerators to find the sum.
The denominator does not change.

Example 1

The denominators are the same.

Add the numerators.

$\dfrac{1}{5}$ $\dfrac{1}{5} + \dfrac{3}{5}$

$+\dfrac{3}{5}$

$\dfrac{4}{5}$

Example 2

The denominators are not the same.

$\dfrac{1}{3}$

$+\dfrac{3}{4}$

Rename both fractions as equivalent fractions having a common denominator.

$\dfrac{1}{3} = \dfrac{1 * 4}{3 * 4} = \dfrac{4}{12}$

$+\dfrac{3}{4} = \dfrac{3 * 3}{4 * 3} = \dfrac{9}{12}$

Add the numerators.

$\dfrac{13}{12}$

$\dfrac{1}{3} + \dfrac{3}{4} = \dfrac{13}{12}$, or $1\dfrac{1}{12}$

Check Your Understanding

Solve the following problems:

1. $\dfrac{4}{7} + \dfrac{2}{7}$ 2. $\dfrac{1}{8} + \dfrac{5}{8}$ 3. $\dfrac{5}{6} + \dfrac{5}{6}$ 4. $\dfrac{1}{3} + \dfrac{1}{4}$

5. $\dfrac{1}{2} + \dfrac{1}{8}$ 6. $\dfrac{2}{3} + \dfrac{1}{6}$ 7. $\dfrac{1}{3} + \dfrac{3}{8}$ 8. $\dfrac{5}{8} + \dfrac{5}{12}$

Write your answers on a separate sheet of paper.

Algorithms for Mixed-Number Addition (with Models)

A mixed number names a whole and a fractional part of a whole. For example, the mixed number $3\frac{1}{3}$ names 3 wholes and $\frac{1}{3}$ of another whole.

When adding mixed numbers, some problem solvers prefer to add the whole numbers first and then the fractions. Others choose the reverse—fractions first and then whole numbers.

Build Understanding

If students need to review the algorithm for fraction addition, refer them to page 25.

Demonstrate how to simplify the mixed number $2\frac{7}{4}$. Draw a diagram on the board showing 2 whole circles, 1 circle divided into 4 equal parts, and $\frac{3}{4}$ of a circle. Explain that this drawing shows 2 wholes and 7 fourths. Then write $2 + \frac{4}{4} + \frac{3}{4}$ below the drawings and show that $2 + \frac{4}{4} + \frac{3}{4}$ is equal to $2 + 1 + \frac{3}{4}$, or $3\frac{3}{4}$.

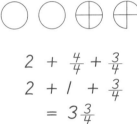

$$2 + \frac{4}{4} + \frac{3}{4}$$
$$2 + 1 + \frac{3}{4}$$
$$= 3\frac{3}{4}$$

Using page 27, explain that students will use their knowledge of fraction addition to solve addition problems having mixed numbers. Then they will rename the sum of each problem if it is not in simplest form. Ask students how the diagram next to $3\frac{6}{4}$ shows the sum of $2\frac{3}{4}$ and $1\frac{3}{4}$. Then have a student explain how the diagram shows that $3\frac{6}{4}$ equals $4\frac{1}{2}$. Use questions like the following to guide students through the examples:

- How do you rename $3\frac{6}{4}$ so that it's in simplest form? *($3\frac{6}{4}$ is equal to $3 + \frac{4}{4} + \frac{2}{4}$, which is equal to $3 + 1 + \frac{2}{4}$, or $4\frac{1}{2}$.)*
- In Example 2, what is a common denominator of $\frac{1}{2}$ and $\frac{2}{3}$? *(6)*
- Does it matter whether you add the whole numbers first or the fractions first? *(No.)*

Error Alert Watch for students who, when simplifying a number like $1\frac{9}{5}$, ignore the whole number and give the answer as $1\frac{4}{5}$ instead of $2\frac{4}{5}$. If necessary, assign extra practice exercises in simplifying mixed numbers.

Check Understanding

Divide the class into groups of 3 and ask each group to solve the problem $2\frac{3}{8} + 4\frac{5}{16}$. Have one member of the group draw a diagram to solve the problem. Have the other members use the algorithm. The group members then compare their answers to make sure they are the same. If they are not the same, have the group members correct the error. Circulate around the room checking students' work. When you are reasonably certain that most of your students understand the algorithm, assign the "Check Your Understanding" exercises at the bottom of page 27. *(See answers in margin.)*

Page 27 Answer Key

1. 8

2. $8\frac{2}{5}$

3. $3\frac{1}{2}$

4. $4\frac{5}{6}$

5. $15\frac{11}{16}$

6. $10\frac{3}{10}$

7. $10\frac{17}{24}$

8. $20\frac{17}{36}$

Algorithms for Mixed-Number Addition (with Models)

One way to add mixed numbers is to add the whole numbers and fractions separately. Check for like denominators before you add the fractional parts. Rename the sum if necessary.

Example 1

$$2\frac{3}{4}$$
$$+\ 1\frac{3}{4}$$
$$\overline{3\frac{6}{4}}$$

Add the fractions and whole numbers.

Rename the sum.

$$3\frac{6}{4} = 3 + \frac{4}{4} + \frac{2}{4}$$
$$= 3 + 1 + \frac{2}{4}$$
$$= 4\frac{2}{4} = 4\frac{1}{2}$$

Example 2

$$3\frac{1}{2}$$
$$+\ 2\frac{2}{3}$$

Rename the fractions so that they have a common denominator.

$$3\frac{3}{6}$$
$$+\ 2\frac{4}{6}$$
$$\overline{5\frac{7}{6}}$$

Add the fractions and whole numbers.

Rename the sum.

$$5\frac{7}{6} = 5 + \frac{6}{6} + \frac{1}{6}$$
$$= 5 + 1 + \frac{1}{6}$$
$$= 6\frac{1}{6}$$

Check Your Understanding

Solve the following problems:

1. $2\frac{1}{3} + 5\frac{2}{3}$

2. $3\frac{4}{5} + 4\frac{3}{5}$

3. $1\frac{5}{8} + 1\frac{7}{8}$

4. $1\frac{7}{12} + 3\frac{1}{4}$

5. $7\frac{3}{8} + 8\frac{5}{16}$

6. $5\frac{1}{2} + 4\frac{4}{5}$

7. $6\frac{7}{8} + 3\frac{5}{6}$

8. $10\frac{5}{9} + 9\frac{11}{12}$

Trade-First Algorithm for Subtraction

The trade-first algorithm for subtraction looks just like the standard algorithm (see pages 36 and 37) when it is completed. The difference is that with the trade-first algorithm, all trading (or regrouping) is carried out before any subtracting begins.

Many students find the trade-first algorithm to be an easy alternative to the switching between trading and subtracting that is required in the traditional algorithm.

Build Understanding

Using pages 29, 30, and 31, explain that with this method of subtracting, students will begin by carrying out all necessary trading until the top number in each column is at least as large as the bottom number. Then students will subtract the numbers in each column (either left-to-right or right-to-left) to find the difference. Use questions like the following to guide students through the examples:

- In the example on page 29, which numbers are in the tens place? *(3 and 7)* Can you remove 7 tens from 3 tens? *(No.)* What trade can you make so that you will be able to remove the 7 tens? *(Trade 1 hundred for 10 tens. After trading, there will be 13 tens, and you can then remove 7 tens.)*

- In the example on page 30, what do the 6 and 13 written above the 7 and 3 show? *(They show that 1 of the 7 hundreds was traded for 10 tens, decreasing the number of hundreds to 6 and increasing the number of tens to 13.)*

- In the example on page 31, can you remove the 7 ones without trading? *(No. You must trade to get more ones. There are no tens to trade for ones. So you must trade one of the hundreds for 10 tens and then trade one of those tens for 10 ones.)*

- Does it matter whether you begin trading and subtracting on the left or on the right? *(No.)*

Error Alert Watch for students who simply subtract the lesser number from the greater number in each column, without thought to whether a trade is needed. More work with models can often help these students.

Check Understanding

Have a volunteer go to the board and solve the problem 215 – 196. Ask the volunteer to explain each step as he or she works. The class should direct questions concerning the problem to the volunteer. When you are reasonably certain that most of your students understand the algorithm, assign the "Check Your Understanding" exercises at the bottom of page 29. For practice of simple problems without models, refer students to page 30. For practice of more difficult problems without models, refer students to page 31. *(See answers in margin.)*

Trade-First Algorithm for Subtraction (with Models)

Use blocks to model the larger number. Trade blocks between the place-value columns as necessary. Trade until the top number in each column is at least as large as the bottom number. Then subtract the numbers to find the difference.

Example

$$432 - 175$$

Model the larger number (432).

Think: Can I remove 7 tens from 3 tens? (no)

Trade 1 hundred for 10 tens.

Think: Can I remove 5 ones from 2 ones? (no)

Trade 1 ten for 10 ones.

After all the trading, the blocks look like this.

Subtract the numbers in each column.

257 is the difference.

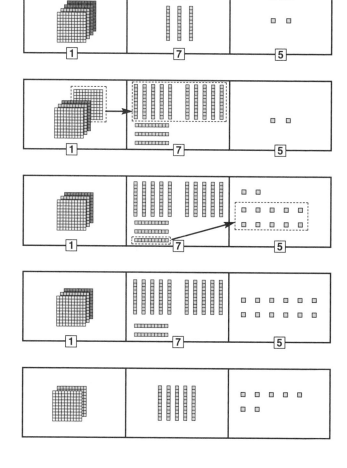

Check Your Understanding

Solve the following problems:

1. 29 − 18

2. 61 − 34

3. 76 − 28

4. 83 − 55

5. 241 − 15

6. 322 − 19

7. 115 − 56

8. 200 − 99

Write your answers on a separate sheet of paper.

Trade-First Algorithm for Subtraction

Look at the numbers in each place-value column. Trade until the top number in each column is at least as large as the bottom number. Then subtract the numbers in each column to find the difference.

$$738 - 452$$

Example

Write the problem in a place-value chart.

100s	10s	1s
7	3	8
− 4	5	2

Think: Can I remove 5 tens from 3 tens? (no)
Trade 1 hundred for 10 tens.
Record the trade.

100s	10s	1s
6 ~~7~~	13 ~~3~~	8
− 4	5	2

Think: Can I remove 2 ones from 8 ones? (yes)
Subtract the numbers in each column.

100s	10s	1s
6 ~~7~~	13 ~~3~~	8
− 4	5	2
2	**8**	**6**

286 is the difference.

Check Your Understanding

Solve the following problems:

1. 51 − 32

2. 93 − 25

3. 66 − 58

4. 303 − 72

5. 831 − 62

6. 427 − 153

7. 759 − 86

8. 580 − 59

Write your answers on a separate sheet of paper.

Trade-First Algorithm for Subtraction

Look at the numbers in each place-value column. Trade until the top number in each column is at least as large as the bottom number. Then subtract the numbers in each column to find the difference.

$$\begin{array}{r} 802 \\ -\ 267 \end{array}$$

Example

Write the problem in a place-value chart.

100s	10s	1s
8	0	2
− 2	6	7

Think: Can I remove 6 tens from 0 tens? (no)
Trade 1 hundred for 10 tens.
Record the trade.

100s	10s	1s
7 8̶	10 0̶	2
− 2	6	7

Think: Can I remove 7 ones from 2 ones? (no)
Trade 1 ten for 10 ones.
Record the trade.

100s	10s	1s
7 8̶	9 1̶0̶ 0̶	12 2̶
− 2	6	7

Subtract the numbers in each column.

100s	10s	1s
7 8̶	9 1̶0̶ 0̶	12 2̶
− 2	6	7

535 is the difference.

| 5 | 3 | 5 |

Check Your Understanding

Solve the following problems:

1. 92 − 68   **2.** 84 − 35   **3.** 938 − 49

4. 782 − 95   **5.** 111 − 92   **6.** 503 − 224

7. 1,340 − 59   **8.** 2,200 − 307

Left-to-Right Algorithm for Subtraction

The left-to-right algorithm for subtraction builds on a skill most people use daily: reading from left to right. The person using this algorithm begins at the far-left side of the problem and subtracts the subtrahend (the lesser number) from the minuend (the greater number) one place-value column at a time until the final difference between the two numbers is reached.

Most students find it helpful to see the subtrahend expressed in expanded notation, and many students find it natural to move from left to right when performing mathematical operations.

Build Understanding

Review expanded notation: Write 2,638 on the board and explain how to write the number in expanded form (2,000 + 600 + 30 + 8). Have students expand the following numbers at their desks: 318; 1,967; 8,049. Ask volunteers to write the answers on the board, and, if necessary, model a few of the numbers using base-10 blocks.

Note: If students seem confused when one or more of the place values are zero, explain two different ways they can handle the situation: Using 8,049 as an example, students can expand the number either as 8,000 + 0 + 40 + 9 or as 8,000 + 40 + 9.

Using page 33, explain that with this method of subtracting, students will begin on the far-left side of the problem and subtract one place-value column at a time until they find the final difference between the minuend (the top number) and the subtrahend (the bottom number). Use questions like the following to guide students through the example (and through other examples you provide):

- Which number will be broken down into its individual place values? *(the subtrahend)*
- What is the greatest place value in the subtrahend?
- How will you subtract the second-greatest place value in the subtrahend? *(Write it in expanded notation and then subtract it from the minuend.)*
- What is the final difference between the minuend and the subtrahend?

Error Alert Make sure students understand that the second subtracted number (60 in the example on page 33) has been "pulled out" from the original subtrahend. If necessary, have students write each subtrahend in expanded notation and then draw an arrow from each part of the expanded notation to its counterpart in the recorded algorithm (the "solution column").

Check Understanding

Write 213 − 148 on the board. Have three volunteers take turns solving each step of the problem to help emphasize the fact that three place values are being subtracted, one at a time, in sequence. Work through as many problems in this way as necessary until you are reasonably certain that most of your students understand the algorithm. Then assign the "Check Your Understanding" exercises at the bottom of page 33. *(See answers in margin.)*

Page 33
Answer Key

1. 223

2. 566

3. 361

4. 211

5. 6,568

6. 768

7. 42,179

8. 4,449

Left-to-Right Algorithm for Subtraction

Write or think of the subtrahend in expanded notation.
Then subtract each part of the subtrahend from the minuend.
Move left to right, one place-value column at a time, until you
find the difference between the two numbers.

Example

$$857 \text{ (minuend)}$$
$$-\ 469 \text{ (subtrahend)}$$

First, write or think of 469 as 400 + 60 + 9.

Then subtract the hundreds. $\longrightarrow$ *(857 – 400)* $\longrightarrow$

$$857$$
$$-\ 400$$
$$457$$

Then subtract the tens. $\longrightarrow$ *(457 – 60)* $\longrightarrow$

$$-\ \ \ 60$$
$$397$$

Then subtract the ones. $\longrightarrow$ *(397 – 9)* $\longrightarrow$

$$-\ \ \ \ \ 9$$

388 is the difference.

$$388$$

Check Your Understanding

Solve the following problems:

1. 317 – 94
2. 582 – 16
3. 640 – 279

4. 835 – 624
5. 7,104 – 536
6. 2,952 – 2,184

7. 43,870 – 1,691
8. 15,033 – 10,584

Counting-Up Algorithm for Subtraction

The counting-up algorithm for subtraction is similar to the process of making change: In both processes, the problem solver counts up from the lesser number to the greater number. The person making a purchase counts up from the amount due to the amount tendered. The person using the counting-up algorithm counts up from the subtrahend (the lesser number) to the minuend (the greater number), records each count-up amount, and then totals all the count-up amounts to find the difference between the minuend and the subtrahend.

Build Understanding

Conduct a brief, oral review of number pairs that add up to 10. (You say "4," and students respond "6.") Then work with number pairs that add up to the next-higher multiple of 10. (You say "37," and students respond "3.") Finally, move on to number pairs that add up to the next-higher 100 or 1,000. (You say "52," and students respond "48"; you say "720," and students respond "280.")

Using page 35, explain that with this method of subtracting, students will, in effect, turn a subtraction problem into an addition problem by "counting up" to find the difference between the two numbers in the problem. Use questions like the following to guide students through the examples:

- Which number will you begin counting up from? *(the subtrahend—the lesser number)*

- How much do you need to add to the number to count to the nearest ten? The nearest hundred? The nearest thousand? The minuend?

- How many numbers do you have to add on and add up in all to get from the subtrahend to the minuend?

- What is the difference between the subtrahend and the minuend?

Error Alert Watch for students who forget how high to count. Remind students that they are to count up only to the greater number in the problem. If it helps them, have students circle the greater number to remind themselves when to stop!

Check Understanding

Divide the class into small groups, and give a different problem to each group: 811 – 609; 335 – 271; 495 – 184; 241 – 39; 572 – 399; 614 – 255. Have each student in each group use the counting-up algorithm to find the solution to his or her group's problem. Then encourage group members to talk the problem through together. If time allows, have one volunteer from each group explain his or her group's solution to the class. Finally, when you are reasonably certain that most of your students understand the algorithm, assign the "Check Your Understanding" exercises at the bottom of page 35. *(See answers in margin.)*

Counting-Up Algorithm for Subtraction

Start with the subtrahend and decide by how much you want to count up first. Count up, recording the "count-up" amount. Continue counting up until you reach the minuend. Then, to find the difference between the subtrahend and the minuend, find the total of all the count-up amounts.

729
− 518

Example 1

Count up from 518 to 729. →

	518
+ 2 →	520
+ 80 →	600
+ 100 →	700
+ 29 →	729
211	

Then total all the count-up amounts.
211 is the difference.

9,438
− 8,167

Example 2

Count up from 8,167 to 9,438. →

	8,167
+ 3 →	8,170
+ 30 →	8,200
+ 800 →	9,000
+ 438 →	9,438
1,271	

Then total all the count-up amounts.
1,271 is the difference.

Check Your Understanding

Solve the following problems:

1. 814 − 631   **2.** 197 − 22   **3.** 555 − 378

4. 6,097 − 4,928   **5.** 7,112 − 4,509   **6.** 8,836 − 2,399

7. 93,744 − 89,964   **8.** 10,115 − 5,730

Write your answers on a separate sheet of paper.

Right-to-Left Algorithm (Standard) for Subtraction

The right-to-left algorithm (standard) for subtraction is the one that is familiar to most adults and many children. A person using this algorithm subtracts from right to left, one place-value column at a time, regrouping as necessary.

The traditional method for teaching this algorithm is to begin with concrete models (such as base-10 blocks) and then gradually move toward the use of symbols (that is, numerals) only.

Build Understanding

Write the following number on the board (leaving out the comma and adding a fair amount of space between the digits): 28,143. (Fifth and sixth grade students might be ready for a larger number, such as 5,092,411, but, again, be sure to omit all commas and add extra spacing between the digits.) Ask a volunteer to read the number. If the student has difficulty, ask the class what might be done to make the number easier to read. Elicit from students the need for one or more commas, and have another volunteer label each place value with a letter abbreviation (Th, H, T, or O) above each digit.

Using page 37, explain that with this method of subtracting, students will begin with the place value on the far right—the ones. Use questions like the following to guide students through the examples:

- What are the first numbers you will work with? *(the ones)*

- As you study the problem, how many times do you think you will have to rename one of the digits?

- How many digits do you think might be in the answer?

Error Alert Watch for students who write the regrouped number over the correct place-value column but forget to cross out the original number. Keep in mind, however, that some students are able to regroup correctly without the aid of visual reminders.

Check Understanding

Make sure students understand what to do when they need to regroup a place value that is a zero. Write the following problem vertically on the board: 701 − 358. Make sure students understand that they must actually regroup the tens place two times. Have a volunteer work through the problem out loud while you write on the board what the student dictates. When you are reasonably certain that most of your students understand the algorithm, assign the "Check Your Understanding" exercises at the bottom of page 37. *(See answers in margin.)*

Right-to-Left Algorithm (Standard) for Subtraction

Start with the ones column, and subtract one column at a time.
Regroup (rename) as necessary.

Example 1

Think: Can I subtract 9 ones from 5 ones? (no)
Regroup the 5 tens and 5 ones as 4 tens and 15 ones.
Then **subtract** 9 ones from 15 ones.

$$\begin{array}{r} \overset{4\ 15}{8\cancel{5}\cancel{5}} \\ -\ 439 \\ \hline 416 \end{array}$$

Think: Can I subtract 3 tens from 4 tens? (yes)
Subtract 3 tens from 4 tens.
Then **subtract** the hundreds.
416 is the difference.

Example 2

Think: Can I subtract 6 ones from 2 ones? (no)
Regroup the 7 hundreds and 0 tens as 6 hundreds and 10 tens. Then regroup the 10 tens and 2 ones as 9 tens and 12 ones.
Then **subtract** 6 ones from 12 ones.

$$\begin{array}{r} \overset{\ \ \ 9}{\overset{6\ 10\ 12}{7\cancel{0}\cancel{2}}} \\ -\ 586 \\ \hline 116 \end{array}$$

Think: Can I subtract 8 tens from 9 tens? (yes)
Subtract 8 tens from 9 tens.
Then **subtract** the hundreds.

116 is the difference.

Check Your Understanding

Solve the following problems:

1. 601 − 27   **2.** 815 − 74   **3.** 529 − 263   **4.** 7,195 − 856

5. 9,113 − 5,089   **6.** 1,248 − 1,199   **7.** 32,084 − 9,176   **8.** 15,643 − 12,897

Write your answers on a separate sheet of paper.

Trade-First Algorithm for Decimal Subtraction

The trade-first algorithm for subtracting whole numbers can easily be applied to the subtraction of decimals. It looks just like the standard algorithm for decimal subtraction (pages 40–41) when it is completed. The difference is that with the trade-first algorithm, all trading is carried out before any subtracting begins.

Build Understanding

If students need to review the whole-number version of this algorithm, refer them to pages 29–31.

Using page 39, explain that with this method of subtracting decimals, students will begin by writing the problem so that the decimal points are aligned vertically. If the subtrahend and the minuend do not have the same number of decimal places, students will add one or more zeros to the end of one of the numbers so that both numbers have the same number of decimal places.

Students then carry out all necessary trading until the top number in each column is at least as large as the bottom number. Finally, students will subtract the numbers in each column. Use questions like the following to guide students through the examples:

- In the example, which numbers are in the tenths place? *(2 and 7)* Can you remove 7 tenths from 2 tenths? *(No.)* What trade can you make so that you will be able to remove the 7 tenths? *(Trade 1 one for 10 tenths. After trading, there will be 12 tenths, and you can then remove 7 tenths.)*

- What do the 5 and 12 written above the 6 and 2 show? *(They show that 1 of the 6 ones was traded for 10 tenths, decreasing the number of ones to 5 and increasing the number of tenths to 12.)*

- Does it matter whether you begin trading and subtracting on the left or the right? *(No.)*

Error Alert Watch for students who have difficulty subtracting a decimal from a whole number. If it helps students, ask them to draw vertical lines to separate the place-value columns and write place-value abbreviations (100s, 10s, 1s, 0.1s, 0.01s, 0.001s) above the columns. Making the line that separates the ones (1s) and the tenths (0.1s) columns thicker might also help students accurately place the decimal point in the answer.

Check Understanding

Have a volunteer go to the board and solve the problem 8 – 3.14. Ask the volunteer to explain each step as he or she works. The class should direct questions concerning the problem to the volunteer. When you are reasonably certain that most of your students understand the algorithm, assign the "Check Your Understanding" exercises at the bottom of page 39. *(See answers in margin.)*

***Page 39
Answer Key***

1. 4.4

2. 1.2

3. 1.82

4. 2.57

5. 0.87

6. 5.449

7. 0.11

8. 8.992

Trade-First Algorithm for Decimal Subtraction

Use what you already know about subtracting whole numbers. Pay attention to the place values of the minuend and subtrahend when you place the decimal point in the difference.

Example

Write the problem in a place-value chart.

$$6.21 \text{ (minuend)}$$
$$- 2.75 \text{ (subtrahend)}$$

	1s	0.1s	0.01s
	6.	2	1
−	2.	7	5

Think: Can I remove 7 tenths from 2 tenths? (no)

	1s	0.1s	0.01s
	5 ~~6.~~	12 ~~2~~	1
−	2.	7	5

Trade 1 one for 10 tenths.

Think: Can I remove 5 hundredths from 1 hundredth? (no)

Trade 1 tenth for 10 hundredths.

	1s	0.1s	0.01s
	5 ~~6.~~	11 ~~12~~ ~~2~~	11 ~~1~~
−	2.	7	5
	3.	4	6

Subtract the numbers in each column.

3.46 is the difference.

3.46

Check Your Understanding

Solve the following problems:

1. $6.3 - 1.9$ **2.** $3.1 - 1.9$ **3.** $6.82 - 5$

4. $4.37 - 1.8$ **5.** $2 - 1.13$ **6.** $5.81 - 0.361$

7. $1.1 - 0.99$ **8.** $9 - 0.008$

Write your answers on a separate sheet of paper.

Right-to-Left Algorithm (Standard) for Decimal Subtraction

The right-to-left algorithm (standard) for subtracting decimals is one that is familiar to most adults and many children. Those who are proficient in using the standard algorithm with whole numbers should be able to apply their knowledge and skills to decimal situations quite easily. The algorithm and the regrouping process are basically the same. Attention to place value is important because the problem solver always subtracts the values of digits one place-value column at a time—whether those digits are tens or tenths, hundreds or hundredths, and so on.

Build Understanding

If students need to review the whole-number version of this algorithm, refer them to page 37.

Using page 41, explain that with this method of subtracting decimals, students will begin by writing the problem so that the decimal points are aligned. Then, if the subtrahend and the minuend do not have the same number of decimal places, students will write zeros at the right so that all numbers have the same number of decimal places.

Students will then subtract as they would with the standard algorithm for subtracting whole numbers. Tell students to begin subtracting on the right and then move one place-value column at a time to the left. Remind students that when they cannot subtract a digit from the one above it, they will need to regroup. Use questions like the following to guide students through the examples:

- In Example 1, what do the 4 and 17 written above the 57 show? *(They show that 57 has been regrouped as 4 tenths and 17 hundredths.)*

- In Example 2, why is 12.7 rewritten as 12.700? *(so that the minuend has the same number of decimal places as the subtrahend)*

- Where do you put the decimal point in your answer? *(in the same place as the decimal points in the problem)*

Error Alert Watch for students who have difficulty subtracting a decimal from a whole number. Some students have no difficulty writing zeros to the right of a number such as 1.3, but do not see 4 as 4.0 or 4.00. If it helps students, ask them to draw vertical lines to separate the place-value columns and have them write place-value abbreviations (100s, 10s, 1s, 0.1s, 0.01s, 0.001s) above the columns. Making the line that separates the ones (1s) and the tenths (0.1s) columns thicker might also help students know where to place the decimal point in the answer.

Check Understanding

Have a volunteer go to the board and solve the problem 7.1 – 0.71. Encourage the student to explain what he or she is doing while working so that the class can follow along. Have students direct their questions to the volunteer, and guide that student in answering as necessary. Repeat the process with 6 – 0.66. When you are reasonably certain that most of your students understand the algorithm, assign the "Check Your Understanding" exercises at the bottom of page 41.
(See answers in margin.)

Page 41
Answer Key

1. 0.4

2. 0.793

3. 3.75

4. 6.36

5. 3.05

6. 0.5

7. 0.79

8. 7.001

Right-to-Left Algorithm (Standard) for Decimal Subtraction

Check to make sure that the numbers are aligned in columns by place value. Subtract from right to left, regrouping if necessary, as you would with whole numbers. Record the decimal point in the sum.

Example 1

$0.57 - 0.38$

Align the decimal points.

Subtract as you would when subtracting whole numbers from right to left.

Regroup as necessary.

Place the decimal point in your answer.

$$
\begin{array}{r}
\overset{\scriptscriptstyle 4\,17}{0.\cancel{5}\cancel{7}} \\
-\,0.38 \\
\hline
\mathbf{0.19}
\end{array}
$$

Example 2

$12.7 - 1.528$

Align the decimal points.

Rewrite 12.7 as 12.700.

Subtract as you would when subtracting whole numbers from right to left.

Regroup as necessary.

Place the decimal point in your answer.

$$
\begin{array}{r}
\overset{\scriptscriptstyle 6\ \cancel{10}10}{12.7\cancel{0}\cancel{0}} \\
-\ \ 1.528 \\
\hline
\mathbf{11.172}
\end{array}
$$

Check Your Understanding

Solve the following problems:

1. $7.2 - 6.8$ **2.** $0.854 - 0.061$ **3.** $7.85 - 4.1$

4. $11.36 - 5$ **5.** $6.2 - 3.15$ **6.** $3 - 2.5$

7. $11 - 10.21$ **8.** $8 - 0.999$

Write your answers on a separate sheet of paper.

Algorithms for Fraction Subtraction (with Models)

Subtracting fractions requires a firm understanding of the meaning of a fraction's numerator (the number of fractional parts at hand) and denominator (the number of fractional parts in the whole) as well as facility in naming equivalent fractions. When two or more fractions have like denominators, the problem solver subtracts the numerators: that is, the problem solver subtracts the number of fractional parts at hand. The number of fractional parts in the whole—the denominator—does not change.

As is the case with adding fractions, subtracting fractions that have unlike denominators requires an additional step. The problem solver must first rename the fractions so that they have like denominators.

Build Understanding

Review the process of finding common multiples and common denominators. Ask students to find common denominators for problems like $\frac{5}{6} - \frac{1}{3}$ and $\frac{3}{4} - \frac{2}{3}$.

Using page 43, explain that when subtracting fractions with different denominators, students will need to find a common multiple of the denominators, or a common denominator. Then, they will rename the fractions as equivalent fractions having common denominators. Remind students that renaming fractions will be easier if they use the smallest common denominator. Use questions like the following to guide students through the examples:

- To subtract fractions having the same denominator, what do you do to the numerators? *(You subtract them.)* What do you do to the denominator? *(Nothing. It stays the same.)*

- In Example 2, what is a common denominator of $\frac{5}{6}$ and $\frac{1}{4}$? *(12)*

- When renaming $\frac{5}{6}$ so that it has a denominator of 12, which number will you multiply by the numerator? *(2, because 6 * 2 = 12)*

Error Alert Watch for students who multiply incorrectly when they find common denominators. Stress the need to multiply both the numerator and the denominator by the same number.

Check Understanding

Divide the class into groups of 3 and ask each group to solve the problem $\frac{1}{2} - \frac{3}{10}$. Have one member of the group draw a diagram of the problem. Have the other members use the algorithm. The group members then compare the answers to make sure they are the same. If they are not the same, have the group members correct the error. Circulate around the room checking students' work. When you are reasonably certain that most of your students understand the algorithm, assign the "Check Your Understanding" exercises at the bottom of page 43. *(See answers in margin.)*

Page 43
Answer Key

1. $\frac{2}{5}$

2. $\frac{1}{2}$

3. $\frac{2}{9}$

4. $\frac{5}{12}$

5. $\frac{1}{8}$

6. $\frac{1}{2}$

7. $\frac{1}{24}$

8. $\frac{1}{48}$

42 Subtraction Algorithms

Algorithms for Fraction Subtraction (with Models)

Check that the addends have like denominators.
Then subtract the numerators to find the difference.
The denominator does not change.

Example 1

$$\frac{6}{7}$$
$$-\frac{2}{7}$$
$$\overline{\frac{4}{7}}$$

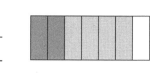

The denominators are the same.

Subtract the numerators.

Example 2

$$\frac{5}{6}$$
$$-\frac{1}{4}$$

The denominators are not the same.

Rename each fraction with a common denominator.

Subtract the numerators.

$$\frac{5}{6} = \frac{5*2}{6*2} = \frac{10}{12}$$
$$-\frac{1}{4} = \frac{1*3}{4*3} = \frac{3}{12}$$
$$\frac{7}{12}$$

Check Your Understanding

Solve the following problems:

1. $\frac{4}{5} - \frac{2}{5}$ 2. $\frac{7}{8} - \frac{3}{8}$ 3. $\frac{7}{9} - \frac{5}{9}$ 4. $\frac{2}{3} - \frac{1}{4}$

5. $\frac{1}{2} - \frac{3}{8}$ 6. $\frac{3}{5} - \frac{1}{10}$ 7. $\frac{7}{8} - \frac{5}{6}$ 8. $\frac{11}{16} - \frac{2}{3}$

Write your answers on a separate sheet of paper.

Algorithms for Mixed-Number Subtraction

A mixed number names one or more wholes and a fractional part of a whole. For example, the mixed number $5\frac{1}{2}$ names 5 wholes and $\frac{1}{2}$ of another whole. Therefore, when problem solvers subtract mixed numbers, they combine the process of subtracting whole numbers and the process of subtracting fractions.

When subtracting mixed numbers, most people prefer to subtract the fractions first because this makes the process a bit less cumbersome when renaming is required. However, problem solvers with good number sense may approach such problems in either way.

Build Understanding

Ask students to draw a picture that shows $2\frac{1}{3}$. On the board, draw the picture on the right and write the fractions below it. Explain that $2\frac{1}{3}$ can be written as $1 + \frac{3}{3} + \frac{1}{3}$, or $1\frac{4}{3}$. Then have students rename $3\frac{1}{5}$ as $2 + \frac{5}{5} + \frac{1}{5} = 2\frac{6}{5}$ and $1\frac{1}{4}$ as $\frac{4}{4} + \frac{1}{4} = \frac{5}{4}$. Give students problems to try on their own.

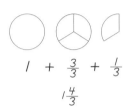

$1 \;+\; \frac{3}{3} \;+\; \frac{1}{3}$

$1\frac{4}{3}$

Using page 45, explain that when subtracting mixed numbers, students will need to rename the minuend (the top number) if the minuend is a whole number or if the fraction part of the minuend is smaller than the fraction part of the subtrahend. In Example 1, students must rename the whole number. Example 2 requires students first to rename the fractions so that they have a common denominator and then rename the minuend so that subtraction is possible. Use questions like the following to guide students through the examples:

- In Example 1, how is the minuend (5) renamed? *(as $4\frac{3}{3}$, so that it has the same denominator as the subtrahend $2\frac{2}{3}$)*

- In Example 2, what is the common denominator of $\frac{1}{3}$ and $\frac{1}{2}$? *(6)*

- In Example 2, why do you need to rename the minuend ($7\frac{2}{6}$) again? *(because $\frac{2}{6}$ in the minuend is smaller than $\frac{3}{6}$ in the subtrahend)*

- How do you rename $7\frac{2}{6}$? *(You rename it as $6 + \frac{6}{6} + \frac{2}{6}$, or $6\frac{8}{6}$.)*

- In Examples 1 and 2, do you need to simplify the difference? *(No. The difference is already in simplest form.)*

Error Alert Watch for students who rename a minuend like $2\frac{1}{5}$ as $2\frac{6}{5}$ instead of $1\frac{6}{5}$. Remind students that they are renaming 2 as $1\frac{5}{5}$. Crossing out the 2 and writing a 1 above it, similar to the way students regroup to subtract whole numbers, might be helpful. Also, make sure students simplify the difference if necessary after they are done subtracting.

Check Understanding

Write $7 - 4\frac{1}{5}$ on the board. Have a volunteer go to the board and solve the problem. Repeat the process with the following problems: $7\frac{2}{5} - 4\frac{1}{5}$, $7\frac{1}{5} - 4\frac{2}{5}$, and $7\frac{1}{5} - 4\frac{1}{3}$. Continue until you are reasonably certain that most of your students understand the algorithms. Then assign the "Check Your Understanding" exercises at the bottom of page 45. *(See answers in margin.)*

Algorithms for Mixed-Number Subtraction

Use what you know about subtracting whole numbers and fractions to subtract mixed numbers. Check for like denominators when you subtract the fractions. Simplify the difference if necessary.

Example 1

$$5 - 2\frac{2}{3}$$

Rename the whole number.

$$4\frac{3}{3}$$

Subtract the whole numbers.

$$-2\frac{2}{3}$$

Subtract the fractions.
Simplify the difference if necessary.

$$2\frac{1}{3}$$

Example 2

$$7\frac{1}{3} - 5\frac{1}{2}$$

Rename the fractions so that they have a common denominator.

$$7\frac{2}{6}$$
$$-5\frac{3}{6}$$

Rename the minuend so that you can subtract.

Subtract the fractions.

$$6\frac{8}{6}$$
$$-5\frac{3}{6}$$

Subtract the whole numbers.
Simplify the difference if necessary.

$$1\frac{5}{6}$$

Check Your Understanding

Solve the following problems:

1. $4 - 1\frac{5}{8}$ **2.** $1 - \frac{3}{5}$ **3.** $3\frac{5}{7} - 1\frac{1}{7}$ **4.** $10\frac{1}{2} - 9\frac{1}{4}$

5. $2\frac{3}{8} - 1\frac{3}{4}$ **6.** $6\frac{1}{3} - 2\frac{5}{6}$ **7.** $1\frac{1}{12} - \frac{2}{3}$ **8.** $8\frac{1}{6} - 6\frac{7}{8}$

Write your answers on a separate sheet of paper.

Partial-Products Algorithm for Multiplication

The partial-products algorithm for multiplication is based on the distributive, or grouping, property of multiplication. A person using this algorithm multiplies each digit of one factor by each of the digits in the other factor, taking into account the place value of each digit. Then the person adds all the partial products to find the total product (each partial product is either a multiplication fact or an extended multiplication fact.)

Students find this algorithm particularly useful for estimating the magnitude of a total product.

Build Understanding

Conduct a quick, oral review of multiples of 10, 100, and 1,000. Call out problems and have the class answer in unison. Begin with simple multiples, such as "2 [10s]," "3 [100s]," and "5 [1,000s]." Avoid saying "2 times 10" because saying (and thinking) "2 tens" emphasizes place value. After a bit of practice, move on to larger multiples of 10, 100, and 1,000, such as 60 [80s], 9 [3,000s], and 40 [500s].

Finally, emphasize the patterns in successive multiples of 10. Have a student come to the board and write the answers to 7 [10s], 7 [100s], 7 [1,000s], and 7 [10,000s]. Ask students to explain the pattern they see emerging. Guide them to conclude that each successive product has one more zero than the product before it.

Using page 47, explain that with this method of multiplying, students can find the partial products in any order. However, starting with the greatest place-value digit in each factor—the one on the far-left side of each factor—will help them keep track of the place values better. Use questions like the following to guide students through each example:

- Which two digits are multiplied to get the first partial product?

- Which partial product is the result of multiplying the two ones digits? *(the last partial product)*

- Can you tell right away how many partial products a problem will have? *(Yes. Observing how many times each digit in one factor must be multiplied by each of the digits in the other factor tells you how many partial products there will be.)*

Error Alert Be sure students know the correct place value of each digit in each factor. For instance, in Example 1 you might notice students multiplying 9 × 4 instead of 9 × 40. If it helps students, ask them to draw vertical lines to separate the place-value columns and have them write place-value abbreviations (100s, 10s, and 1s) above the columns.

Check Understanding

Write 637 * 18 on the board and solve it using the partial-products algorithm. Then have a volunteer or two come to the board, point to each pair of digits that were multiplied to produce each partial product, and explain the value of each of those digits. Do as many examples in this way as necessary, until you are reasonably certain that most of your students understand the algorithm. Then assign the "Check Your Understanding" exercises at the bottom of page 47. For practice of more difficult problems, refer to pages 48 and 49. *(See answers in margin.)*

Partial-Products Algorithm for Multiplication

Multiply each digit in the bottom factor by each digit in the top factor. Then add all of the partial products to find the total product.

Example 1

	100s	10s	1s	
	2	**4**	**5**	(factor)
*			**9**	(factor)

Multiply 9 × 200. →	1	8	0	0
Multiply 9 × 40. →		3	6	0
Multiply 9 × 5. → +			4	5
Add the partial products. →	**2,**	**2**	**0**	**5** (product)

Example 2

	100s	10s	1s	
	7	**4**	**2**	(factor)
*			**5**	(factor)

Multiply 5 × 700. →	3	5	0	0
Multiply 5 × 40. →		2	0	0
Multiply 5 × 2. → +			1	0
Add the partial products. →	**3,**	**7**	**1**	**0** (product)

Check Your Understanding

Solve the following problems:

1. 342 × 6   **2.** 903 × 4   **3.** 654 × 9

4. 793 × 5   **5.** 587 × 7   **6.** 464 × 3

7. 966 × 8   **8.** 8,527 × 5

Write your answers on a separate sheet of paper.   **Multiplication Algorithms 47**

Partial-Products Algorithm for Multiplication

Multiply each digit in the bottom factor by each digit in the top factor. Then add all of the partial products to find the total product.

Example 1

		10s	1s	
		5	**6**	(factor)
*		**8**	**2**	(factor)

Multiply 80 × 50. →	4	0	0	0
Multiply 80 × 6. →		4	8	0
Multiply 2 × 50. →		1	0	0
Multiply 2 × 6. → +			1	2
Add the partial products. →	**4,**	**5**	**9**	**2** (product)

Example 2

		10s	1s	
		9	**4**	(factor)
*		**7**	**6**	(factor)

Multiply 70 × 90. →	6	3	0	0
Multiply 70 × 4. →		2	8	0
Multiply 6 × 90. →		5	4	0
Multiply 6 × 4. → +			2	4
Add the partial products. →	**7,**	**1**	**4**	**4** (product)

Check Your Understanding

Solve the following problems:

1. 45 × 78   **2.** 89 × 56   **3.** 67 × 92

4. 56 × 75   **5.** 59 × 48   **6.** 91 × 87

7. 64 × 95   **8.** 673 × 49

Write your answers on a separate sheet of paper.

Partial-Products Algorithm for Multiplication

Multiply each digit in the bottom factor by each digit in the top factor. Then add all of the partial products to find the total product.

Example

	100s	10s	1s	
	7	**5**	**2**	(factor)
*		**4**	**6**	(factor)

Multiply 40 × 700. →	2	8	0	0	0
Multiply 40 × 50. →		2	0	0	0
Multiply 40 × 2. →				8	0
Multiply 6 × 700. →		4	2	0	0
Multiply 6 × 50. →			3	0	0
Multiply 6 × 2. → +				1	2
Add the partial products. →	**3**	**4,**	**5**	**9**	**2**	(product)

Check Your Understanding

Solve the following problems:

1. 368 × 23   **2.** 604 × 56   **3.** 974 × 21

4. 834 × 67   **5.** 775 × 93   **6.** 485 × 39

7. 789 × 55   **8.** 593 × 347

Write your answers on a separate sheet of paper.

Lattice Algorithm for Multiplication

The lattice algorithm for multiplication has been traced to India, where it was in use before A.D. 1100. It derives its name from the lattice within which the person using the algorithm writes each partial product (see facing page). The problem solver finds the final product by adding all the numerals along each of the diagonals within the lattice.

Many Everyday Mathematics *students find this particular multiplication algorithm to be one of their favorites. It helps them keep track of all the partial products without having to write extra zeros—and it helps them practice their multiplication facts.*

Build Understanding

Introduce the lattice algorithm for multiplication by saying that this is a multiplication method in which the numbers are placed around and within a lattice—a special kind of grid in which the dotted-line "rails" within the cells help form diagonals. Invite students to speculate about why a lattice might be a good way to organize a multiplication problem. Help students realize that a lattice can help the problem solver keep track of the many digits that result from the multiplication of two multidigit factors.

Using page 51, explain that with this method of multiplying, students will be multiplying one digit of each factor by one digit of the other factor and recording each partial product within a cell in the grid. Use questions like the following to guide students through the example (and through other examples you provide):

- Which two numbers are being multiplied? *(The numbers written along the top of the lattice and the outer right side of the lattice. In the example, the two numbers being multiplied are 35 and 26.)*

- Which two-digit number is written in the upper right-hand cell? *(The number that is the product of the two digits along the outside, upper right-hand corner of the lattice. In the example, the two-digit number in the upper right-hand cell is 10—the product of 2 and 5.)*

- Where do you start when adding the numbers inside the lattice? *(You begin with the bottom right-hand corner and work diagonal by diagonal toward the upper left-hand corner.)*

Error Alert Be sure that students enter 0 in the top half of a cell when the product is less than 10. And, as students add the numbers within each diagonal, be certain that they are regrouping correctly: They must regroup each tens digit up to the top of the next diagonal.

Check Understanding

Have a few volunteers demonstrate this algorithm on the board. Guide their descriptions when necessary and demonstrate a couple of extra problems yourself. When you are reasonably certain that most of your students understand the algorithm, assign the "Check Your Understanding" exercises at the bottom of page 51. *(See answers in margin.)*

Page 51 Answer Key

1. 308

2. 792

3. 2,340

4. 3,362

5. 3,796

6. 2,688

7. 17,595

8. 488,592

Lattice Algorithm for Multiplication

Write one factor along the top outside of the grid, one digit per cell. Write the other factor along the outer right side of the grid, one digit per cell. Begin with the first digit from the side factor, and multiply each digit in the top factor by each digit in the side factor. Record each answer in its own cell, placing the tens digit in the upper half of the cell and the ones digit in the bottom half of the cell. Then add along each diagonal—and record any regroupings as shown below.

Example

35 × 26

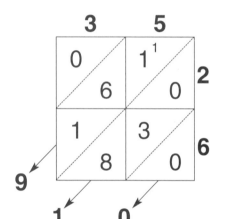

Multiply 2 × 5. **Record** the product in the upper right-hand cell.

Multiply 2 × 3. **Record** the product in the upper left-hand cell.

Multiply 6 × 5. **Record** the product in the lower right-hand cell.

Multiply 6 × 3. **Record** the product in the lower left-hand cell.

Add along each diagonal beginning with the bottom, right diagonal. Work toward the upper left diagonal. **Regroup** each tens digit to the top of the next diagonal (to help you remember to add that digit).

The product of **35** and **26** is **910**.

Check Your Understanding

Solve the following problems:

1. 14 × 22

2. 44 * 18

3. 65 * 36

4. 82 * 41

5. 73 × 52

6. 96 * 28

7. 391 * 45

8. 624 × 783

Write your answers on a separate sheet of paper.

Short Algorithm (Standard) for Multiplication (with Models)

The short algorithm (standard) for multiplication is the one that is familiar to most adults and many children. A person using this algorithm multiplies from right to left, regrouping as necessary.

The traditional method for teaching this algorithm is to begin with models (such as base-10 blocks), using them to demonstrate the regrouping process.

Build Understanding

Divide the class into small groups and distribute base-10 blocks to each group. Ask each group to use the least number of blocks to represent the number 26. (They should show 2 tens and 6 ones.) Then write the problem 26×2 on the board, and ask the groups to model the problem, using the least number of blocks to show the product. Check to see how many students traded 10 ones for 1 ten, which would give them a total of 5 tens and 2 ones.

Using page 53, explain that with this method of multiplying, students will begin multiplying the ones digits. Use questions like the following to guide students through the example:

- Why does the first step of the model have 3 sets of blocks with 2 tens and 7 ones in each? *(because the top factor, 27, has 2 tens and 7 ones, —and we're multiplying those 2 tens and 7 ones 3 times)*

- Why are the 21 ones grouped together in the first step of the model? *(to show that we multiply the ones digits first)*

- In the second step of the model, why have the 21 ones been replaced by 2 tens and 1 one? *(to show the renaming, or regrouping, that is taking place)*

Error Alert Watch for students who misalign the products under the factors. If it helps students, allow them to draw vertical lines between the place-value columns, and show them how to extend the lines below the problem so that the lines will help guide them as they record the answer.

Check Understanding

Divide the class into pairs, designating a "writer" and a "solver" within each partnership. Give partners problems to solve together. The "solver" should dictate the solution to the "writer." You might use any of the following problems (and add some of your own as needed): 13 * 4; 85 * 2; 61 * 7; 11 * 5; 22 * 3; 49 * 6. Explain that the "writer" should challenge the "solver" whenever the "writer" thinks a direction is incorrect. Then have partners switch tasks and work through a second problem. When you are reasonably certain that most of your students understand the algorithm, assign the "Check Your Understanding" exercises at the bottom of page 53. *(See answers in margin.)*

Short Algorithm (Standard) for Multiplication (with Models)

Use blocks to model the problem. Multiply from right to left.
Then find the total.

Example

Multiply the ones.
(3 × 7 = 21 ones.)

$$\begin{array}{r} 27 \\ \times\ 3 \\ \hline \end{array}$$

Rename 21 ones as
2 tens and 1 one.

$$\begin{array}{r} \overset{2}{2}7 \\ \times\ 3 \\ \hline 1 \end{array}$$

Multiply the tens.
(3 × 2 tens = 6 tens.)

$$\begin{array}{r} \overset{2}{2}7 \\ \times\ 3 \\ \hline 1 \end{array}$$

Add the remaining tens.
(6 tens + 2 tens = 8 tens.)

$$\begin{array}{r} \overset{2}{2}7 \\ \times\ 3 \\ \hline 81 \end{array}$$

The product of **3** and **27** is **81.**

Check Your Understanding

Solve the following problems:

1. 64 × 3　　　　**2.** 56 * 8　　　　**3.** 97 × 5

4. 505 * 3　　　　**5.** 291 * 4　　　　**6.** 137 × 49

7. 816 * 4　　　　**8.** 495 * 3

Short Algorithm (Standard) for Multiplication

The short algorithm (standard) for multiplication is the one that is familiar to most adults and many children. A person using this algorithm multiplies from right to left, regrouping as necessary.

The traditional method for teaching this algorithm is to begin with models (such as base-10 blocks) and then gradually move toward the use of symbols (that is, numerals) only.

Build Understanding

Since students will need a sharp eye for place value to succeed with this algorithm, conduct a basic-facts review—with a place-value twist. Have students take out their slates and chalk, or paper and pencils. On their slates, have them copy the chart shown in the margin. Tell them that you will call out problems and that they should write the answers on their slates with the digits written correctly in the chart.

Ask a volunteer to read her or his answer and identify the value of each digit (for example: "72; 7 tens and 2 ones"). After reviewing some of the basic multiplication facts, expand the review to include multiples of ten. Use such problems as 30 * 8; 60 * 4; 200 * 7; and 500 * 5. Make sure students expand their place-value charts to accommodate their 3- and 4-digit answers.

Using page 55, explain that with this method of multiplying, students will begin with the ones digit in the bottom factor. Use questions such as the following to guide students through the example (and through other examples you provide):

- Will you begin multiplying with the digits on the right or on the left? *(on the right)*

- What is the correct method for recording each individual product? *(If the product has one digit, align it in the correct column under the two factors. If the product has two digits, align the right digit below the two factors, in the correct column, and regroup the left digit at the top of the next place-value column to the left. If there are no columns to the left, then record the 2-digit answer.)*

Error Alert Watch for students who skip a digit when they multiply a 3-digit number by a 2-digit number. Have students use their index fingers to point to each digit in the top factor as they work. This method may help ensure that students multiply every digit in the bottom factor by every digit in the top factor.

Check Understanding

Divide students into pairs. Have them solve the problem 572 * 43. Tell them to write neatly, and then have them exchange papers with their partners. Direct students to check each other's problems. If they find a mistake, ask them to identify the mistake. When you are reasonably certain that most of your students understand the algorithm, assign the "Check Your Understanding" exercises at the bottom of page 55. *(See answers in margin.)*

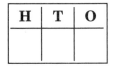

H	T	O

Page 55 Answer Key

1. 432

2. 210

3. 558

4. 11,051

5. 7,975

6. 36,064

7. 19,203

8. 57,908

Short Algorithm (Standard) for Multiplication

First, multiply the ones digit in the bottom factor by the ones digit in the top factor. Record any regrouping at the top of the next place-value column. Then, multiply each of the remaining digits in the bottom factor by each of the remaining digits in the top factor, moving from right to left. Finally, if you have partial products, add them to find the total product.

Example

Multiply 5 ones by 4 ones. *(20 ones)*
Rename 20 ones as 2 tens and 0 ones.
Record the 0 ones in the ones column.
Record the 2 tens at the top of the tens column.

$$\begin{array}{r} {}^{2} \\ 34 \\ *\ 15 \\ \hline 0 \end{array}$$

Multiply 5 ones by 3 tens. *(15 tens)*
Add 2 tens. *(15 tens + 2 tens = 17 tens)*
Record the 17 tens.

$$\begin{array}{r} {}^{2} \\ 34 \\ *\ 15 \\ \hline 170 \end{array}$$

Multiply 1 ten by 4 ones *(40)* and 1 ten by 3 tens *(300)*.
Record 340.

$$\begin{array}{r} {}^{2} \\ 34 \\ *\ 15 \\ \hline 170 \\ +\ 340 \\ \hline \mathbf{510} \end{array}$$

Add the partial products to find the final product.

Check Your Understanding

Solve the following problems:

1. 54 * 8   **2.** 70 × 3   **3.** 62 * 9   **4.** 257 * 43

5. 319 × 25   **6.** 784 * 46   **7.** 519 × 37   **8.** 467 * 124

Partial-Products Algorithm for Decimal Multiplication

The partial-products algorithm for multiplication can be applied to decimal multiplication. The only difference is that the decimal place value will be ignored until the end solution is recorded. Students find this algorithm particularly helpful for estimating the location of the decimal point. The challenge is to understand where to correctly position the decimal point in the product, a process that requires greater number sense and estimation skills than required in whole number multiplication.

Methods that improve students' understanding of decimal multiplication include using models (base-10 blocks) to show repeated addition or groupings, using calculators to look for patterns in the decimals, and rounding factors to find a reasonable estimate, or magnitude estimate, for the product.

Build Understanding

If students need to review the whole-number version of this algorithm, refer them to pages 47–49.

Review the process of making a magnitude estimate of the product in a decimal multiplication problem. Write the problem 3.8 * 4.3 on the board. Explain that each of these numbers can be rounded to 4. Since 4 * 4 = 16, the product will be in the tens. Have students practice finding magnitude estimates for problems like this on their own. Provide opportunities for students to share strategies.

Using page 57, explain that students should first make a magnitude estimate for the answer. Then they should multiply just as they would with the whole-number version of the partial-products algorithm. Finally, they should use their magnitude estimate to help them place the decimal point in the answer. Use questions like the following to guide students through each example:

- Which two digits are multiplied to get the first partial product?

- How can you tell how many partial products you will end up with? *(Observing how many times each digit in one factor must be multiplied by each digit in the other factor tells how many partial products there will be.)*

Page 57 Answer Key

1. 29.88

2. 33.32

3. 24.284

4. 62.175

5. 33.12

6. 19.72

7. 53.82

8. 48.0501

- What is a reasonable estimate for the answer of this problem?

- Based on the estimate, where will you place the decimal point?

Error Alert Be sure students remember to ignore the decimal points as they work the problem using the partial-products algorithm for whole numbers. Once the total for the partial product is recorded, check to see that students use their magnitude estimate to help them place the decimal point correctly in the answer. If needed, require students to record their magnitude estimate so you can check their understanding.

Check Understanding

Write 4.5 * 32 on the board and solve it using the partial-products algorithm, ignoring the decimal point. Then have a volunteer or two come to the board and point to each pair of digits that were multiplied to produce each partial product. Have students also explain how they would use a magnitude estimate for the product to help them decide where to place the decimal point. Repeat the process until you are reasonably certain that most of your students understand the algorithm. Then assign the "Check Your Understanding" exercises at the bottom of page 57. *(See answers in margin.)*

Partial-Products Algorithm for Decimal Multiplication

First, make a magnitude estimate. Next, multiply each digit in the bottom factor by each digit in the top factor. Then add all of the partial products. Use your magnitude estimate to correctly place the decimal point in the product.

Example

Step 1: Make a magnitude estimate.
- Round 7.4 to 7 and 6.9 to 7.
- Since 7 * 7 = 49, the product will be in the tens.

$$7.4 * 6.9$$

Step 2: Multiply as you would for whole numbers.

	74 (factor)
	× 69 (factor)
Multiply 60 * 70. →	4200
Multiply 60 * 4. →	240
Multiply 9 * 70. →	630
Multiply 9 * 4. →	+ 36
Add the partial products. →	5106

Step 3: Place the decimal point correctly in the answer. Since the magnitude estimate is in the tens, the product must be in the tens.

$$7.4 * 6.9 = 51.06 \text{ (product)}$$

Check Your Understanding

Solve the following problems:

1. 8.3 * 3.6   **2.** 6.8 * 4.9   **3.** 5.2 * 4.67   **4.** 8.29 * 7.5

5. 7.2 * 4.6   **6.** 5.8 * 3.4   **7.** 6.9 * 7.8   **8.** 6.09 * 7.89

Write your answers on a separate sheet of paper.

Lattice Algorithm for Decimal Multiplication

The lattice algorithm for multiplication, a favorite of many Everyday Mathematics *students, can be adapted and applied to decimal multiplication. The challenge is to understand where to correctly position the decimal point in the product, a process that requires greater number sense and estimation skills than required in decimal addition and subtraction.*

Provide opportunities for students to explore decimal multiplication before trying to apply familiar multiplication algorithms. Methods that improve students' understanding of decimal multiplication include using models (base-10 blocks) to show repeated addition or groupings, using calculators to look for patterns in the decimals, and rounding factors to find a reasonable range for the product.

Build Understanding

If students need to review the whole-number version of this algorithm, refer them to page 51.

Review the process of finding a reasonable range for the answer to a multiplication problem. Explain that the answer to $2.8 * 3.2$ is going to be greater than 6 (2×3) because 2.8 is greater than 2 and 3.2 is greater than 3. The answer to $2.8 * 3.2$ is going to be less than 12 (3×4) because 2.8 is less than 3 and 3.2 is less than 4. So, $2.8 * 3.2$ is going to be between 6 and 12. Have students practice finding ranges for a few problems like this on their own.

Using page 59, explain that students multiply just as they do with the whole-number version of the lattice multiplication. Then, they find a reasonable range for the answer and use the range to place the decimal point. Use questions like the following to guide students through the example:

- Which two numbers are being multiplied? *(The numbers written along the outside top of the lattice and the outer right side of the lattice.)*

Page 59 Answer Key

- Which two-digit number goes in the lower left-hand cell? *(The product of the upper left-hand number and the lower right-hand number. In the example, the two-digit number in the lower-left hand cell is 06—the product of 6 and 1.)*

- Why do you need to find a reasonable range for the answer? *(to know where to place the decimal point)*

- How do you find a reasonable range for the answer? *(You round both of the numbers down and multiply to get a low estimate; then you round both of the numbers up and multiply to get a high estimate. The range is between the low estimate and the high estimate.)*

Error Alert Be sure that students enter 0 in the top half of a cell when the product is less than 10. Watch for students who do not add correctly along each diagonal: Students must regroup each tens digit up to the top of the next diagonal.

Check Understanding

Have a volunteer go to the board and use lattice multiplication to solve $1.4 * 6.2$. Encourage the student to explain what he or she is doing while working so that the class can follow along. Have students direct their questions to the volunteer, and guide that student in answering as necessary. When you are reasonably certain that most of your students understand the algorithm, assign the "Check Your Understanding" exercises at the bottom of page 59. *(See answers in margin.)*

Page 59 Answer Key

1. 11.61

2. 5.58

3. 49.4

4. 31.62

5. 91.3

6. 403.2

7. 62.7

8. 9.702

Lattice Algorithm for Decimal Multiplication

Use what you already know about multiplying whole numbers using the lattice algorithm. To correctly place the decimal point in the product, estimate the product. You can also use the method explained below for placing the decimal point.

Example $6.5 * 3.1$

Multiply as you would with whole numbers.

Multiply $3 * 5$. Record the product in the upper right-hand cell.

Multiply $3 * 6$. Record the product in the upper left-hand cell.

Multiply $1 * 5$. Record the product in the lower right-hand cell.

Multiply $1 * 6$. Record the product in the lower left-hand cell.

Add along each diagonal, starting at the bottom right. Regroup as necessary.

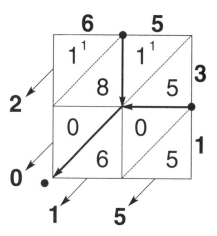

To place the decimal point, find the intersection of the decimal points along the horizontal and vertical lines; then slide it down its diagonal.

$6.5 * 3.1 = 20.15$

Check Your Understanding

Solve the following problems:

1. $2.7 * 4.3$ **2.** 3.1×1.8 **3.** 7.6×6.5

4. $9.3 * 3.4$ **5.** 83×1.1 **6.** $5.6 * 72$

7. 11×5.7 **8.** $9.9 * 0.98$

Write your answers on a separate sheet of paper.

Short Algorithm (Standard) for Decimal Multiplication

The short algorithm (standard) for decimal multiplication is one that is familiar to most adults and many children. The algorithm is applied to decimals just as one would apply it to whole numbers, with the additional challenge of understanding where to place the decimal point in the product. To be successful, students must apply their number sense and their estimation skills.

Methods that improve students' understanding of decimal multiplication include using models (base-10 blocks) to show repeated addition or groupings, using calculators to look for patterns in the decimals, and rounding factors to find a reasonable range for the product.

Build Understanding

If students need to review the whole-number version of this algorithm, refer them to page 55.

Review the process of estimating products of decimals. Write 2.8 * 1.3 on the board and ask students to estimate the answer. Guide students to see that since 2.8 is almost 3, and 1.3 is between 1 and 2, the answer will be between 3 (3 * 1) and 6 (3 * 2). Then have students find the range for the problem 30.8 * 4.7.

Using page 61, explain that with this method of decimal multiplication, students will multiply the factors as if they were whole numbers and then estimate to find a range for the answer, using their number sense to place the decimal point. Use questions like the following to guide students through the example:

- What do you need to do first? *(Rewrite the problem using whole numbers. In the example, 4.8 * 7.3 should be written as 48 * 73.)*
- Why must 4.8 * 7.3 be greater than 28 (4 * 7)? *(4.8 is greater than 4, and 7.3 is greater than 7, so 4.8 * 7.3 is greater than 4 * 7.)*
- Why must 4.8 * 7.3 be less than 40 (5 * 8)? *(4.8 is less than 5, and 7.3 is less than 8, so 4.8 * 7.3 is less than 5 * 8.)*

- Where do you place the decimal point in 3504 so that the product is between 28 and 40? *(between the 5 and the 0: 35.04)*
- What is a "shortcut" method to use when figuring out where to place the decimal point? *(Count the total number of decimal places in both factors. It should be the same as the number of decimal places in the product.)*

Error Alert Watch for students who incorrectly place the decimal point. Remind students that they can always simply count the total number of decimal places in both factors to determine how many decimal places should be in the product.

Check Understanding

Have a student make up a problem that he or she considers easy and write it on the board. Then have a volunteer go to the board and solve the problem. Repeat the process until you are reasonably certain that most of your students understand the algorithm. Then assign the "Check Your Understanding" exercises at the bottom of page 61. *(See answers in margin.)*

Page 61 Answer Key

1. 9.25
2. 51.84
3. 25.74
4. 54.29
5. 187
6. 1,476.3
7. 2,851.2
8. 13.448

Short Algorithm (Standard) for Decimal Multiplication

Use what you already know about multiplying whole numbers using the short algorithm (standard). Round the factors and multiply mentally to find a sensible range for the product. Use this sensible range to help you correctly place the decimal point in the product.

Example

$4.8 * 7.3$

Multiply as you would with whole numbers.

Estimate to place the decimal point in the answer.

- 4.8 is between 4 and 5.
- 7.3 is between 7 and 8.
- The product of 4.8 and 7.3 is between 28 ($4 * 7$) and 40 ($5 * 8$).
- 35.04 is between 28 and 40.

$$
\begin{array}{r}
2 \\
48 \\
\times \quad 73 \\
\hline
144 \\
+ \quad 3360 \\
\hline
3504
\end{array}
$$

or

Count the total number of decimal places in both factors to place the decimal point in the answer. (The total number of decimal places in both factors will equal the number of decimal places in the product.)

$4.8 * 7.3 = 35.04$

Check Your Understanding

Solve the following problems:

1. $3.7 * 2.5$ **2.** 8.1×6.4 **3.** 3.3×7.8

4. $6.1 * 8.9$ **5.** 34×5.5 **6.** $70.3 * 21$

7. 891×3.2 **8.** $6.56 * 2.05$

Write your answers on a separate sheet of paper.

Algorithms for Fraction Multiplication

When the factors are easy to work with, an area model is a good way to find the product of two fractions. This method is useful as a first multiplication method for students because it helps them visualize the multiplication process. It also helps students relate the values of the denominators of the factors to the value of the denominator of the product.

Once students have experience with the area model and an understanding of fraction multiplication, they are ready to apply the Multiplication of Fractions Property. When doing so, problem solvers multiply the numerators of the factors and multiply the denominators of the factors to name the numerator and denominator in the product.

Build Understanding

Using page 63, show students the area model for multiplying fractions. The area model is a good representation of what it means to multiply two fractions. The first diagram in Example 1 shows one fraction, $\frac{3}{4}$, and the second diagram shows $\frac{1}{3}$ of $\frac{3}{4}$. Spend time with the area model before moving on to the algorithm that uses the Multiplication of Fractions Property (Example 2).

Use questions like the following to guide students through the examples:

- How do you find $\frac{3}{4}$ of a region? *(You divide a region into 4 equal parts and shade 3 of them.)*
- How do you find $\frac{1}{3}$ of a region? *(You divide a region into 3 equal parts and shade 1 part.)*
- What part of the diagram shows $\frac{1}{3} * \frac{3}{4}$? *(the region where the shading overlaps)*
- In Example 2, which numbers do you multiply to find the product of the two fractions? *(You multiply one numerator by the other numerator. You multiply one denominator by the other denominator.)*

Error Alert Watch for students who incorrectly identify the product on an area model. Different-color markers might help students see the overlap clearly. Make sure students using the Multiplication of Fractions Property multiply both the numerators and the denominators.

Check Understanding

Divide the class into groups of 2. Give students this problem to solve: $\frac{1}{4} * \frac{2}{3}$. Have one partner draw an area model to solve the problem. Have the other partner use the Multiplication of Fractions Property algorithm to solve the problem. The partners then compare the answers to make sure they are the same. If they are not the same, they correct their work. Then have partners switch roles to solve this problem: $\frac{2}{5} \times \frac{1}{2}$. Circulate around the room checking students' work. When you are reasonably certain that most of your students understand the area-model and Multiplication of Fractions Property algorithms, assign the "Check Your Understanding" exercises at the bottom of page 63. *(See answers in margin.)*

Page 63
Answer Key

1. $\frac{1}{4}$

2. $\frac{7}{20}$

3. $\frac{3}{10}$

4. $\frac{2}{7}$

5. $\frac{1}{3}$

6. $\frac{10}{27}$

7. $\frac{6}{35}$

8. $\frac{1}{8}$

Algorithms for Fraction Multiplication

An area model and the Multiplication of Fractions Property are two methods you can use to multiply fractions.

Example 1 **Area Model**

$$\frac{1}{3} * \frac{3}{4}$$

Show $\frac{3}{4}$ of a region shaded.

Show $\frac{1}{3}$ of that region shaded.

The portion that overlaps shows $\frac{1}{3}$ of $\frac{3}{4}$.

$$\frac{1}{3} * \frac{3}{4} = \frac{3}{12}, \text{ or } \frac{1}{4}$$

Example 2 **Multiplication of Fractions Property**

$$\frac{5}{6} * \frac{1}{2}$$

Multiply the numerators.

Multiply the denominators.

$$\frac{5}{6} * \frac{1}{2} = \frac{5 * 1}{6 * 2} = \frac{5}{12}$$

Check Your Understanding

Solve the following problems:

1. $\frac{3}{8} * \frac{2}{3}$ **2.** $\frac{1}{2} * \frac{7}{10}$ **3.** $\frac{2}{5} * \frac{3}{4}$

4. $\frac{1}{3} * \frac{6}{7}$ **5.** $\frac{5}{9} * \frac{3}{5}$ **6.** $\frac{5}{9} * \frac{2}{3}$

7. $\frac{3}{5} * \frac{4}{14}$ **8.** $\frac{3}{14} * \frac{7}{12}$

Write your answers on a separate sheet of paper.

Algorithms for Mixed-Number Multiplication

The algorithms people choose for multiplying mixed numbers depend on the values of the factors and how easy they are to work with. By renaming both factors as fractions, problem solvers can proceed directly with fraction multiplication. This method is surely accurate and is the one typically taught to students. However, when one of the factors is a whole number and the other a mixed number, it may be more efficient to apply the distributive property— multiplying each part of the mixed-number factor by the whole-number factor.

Build Understanding

Review the process of renaming a mixed number as a fraction. Write $3\frac{1}{3}$ on the board and explain how to rename this mixed number as a fraction ($\frac{10}{3}$). Then have students rename the following mixed numbers at their desks: $2\frac{1}{4}$; $3\frac{2}{3}$; $1\frac{1}{8}$. Ask volunteers to write the answers on the board.

Using page 65, explain that there are two ways to multiply mixed numbers. In Example 1, both factors are mixed numbers. Students first rename each number as a fraction and then use the Multiplication of Fractions Property to multiply the fractions. In Example 2, one of the factors is a whole number. Students could use the same method they use for multiplying mixed numbers, but the method shown in Example 2 often results in simpler computation. This method uses the distributive property: students consider the mixed number as two parts, a whole number and a fraction, and each of these parts is multiplied by the whole number. Students then add the partial products. Use questions like the following to guide students through the examples:

- What is $2\frac{1}{2}$ renamed as a fraction? ($\frac{5}{2}$)
- Why is $\frac{20}{6}$ equal to $3\frac{2}{6}$? *(20 ÷ 6 = 3 R2. The whole-number part of the quotient is the whole-number part of the mixed number; the remainder is the numerator of the fraction part of the mixed number; and the divisor is the denominator of the fraction part of the mixed number.)*
- What two steps do you follow to multiply 5 by $3\frac{1}{4}$? *(5 × 3 and 5 × $\frac{1}{4}$)*

Error Alert Watch for students who have difficulty writing mixed numbers as fractions. Many students multiply the whole-number part of the mixed number by the denominator of the fraction part but forget to add the numerator of the fraction. For example, these students might rename $2\frac{1}{3}$ as $\frac{6}{3}$. Also, watch for students who multiply the partial products instead of adding them.

Check Understanding

Write $8 \times 3\frac{2}{7}$ on the board. Have two volunteers go to the board and work through this problem. Ask one volunteer to use the standard algorithm, and ask the other to use the algorithm shown in Example 2. Students should get the same result using the two algorithms, but they will notice that the computation using the second algorithm is simpler. When you are reasonably certain that most of your students understand both algorithms, assign the "Check Your Understanding" exercises at the bottom of page 65. *(See answers in margin.)*

Page 65 Answer Key

1. $1\frac{7}{8}$

2. $3\frac{4}{15}$

3. $4\frac{2}{9}$

4. 15

5. $25\frac{3}{5}$

6. 57

7. $5\frac{5}{16}$

8. $10\frac{13}{24}$

Algorithms for Mixed-Number Multiplication

Here are two ways to multiply mixed numbers. The method you use usually depends on the values of the factors.

Example 1   Change-to-Fractions Algorithm (Standard)

$$2\tfrac{1}{2} * 1\tfrac{1}{3}$$

Rename the mixed numbers as fractions.

$$\tfrac{5}{2} * \tfrac{4}{3}$$

Multiply the fractions.

$$\frac{5 * 4}{2 * 3} = \frac{20}{6}$$

Rename the product as a mixed number. Simplify the product if necessary.

$$\frac{20}{6} = 3\tfrac{2}{6} = 3\tfrac{1}{3}$$

$$2\tfrac{1}{2} * 1\tfrac{1}{3} = 3\tfrac{1}{3}$$

Example 2   Multiplying a Whole Number and a Mixed Number

$$5 * 3\tfrac{1}{4}$$

Multiply the whole number by the whole-number part of the mixed number.

$$5 * (3 + \tfrac{1}{4})$$

Multiply the whole number by the fraction part of the mixed number.

$$(5 * 3) + (5 * \tfrac{1}{4})$$

Add the partial products. Simplify the product if necessary.

$$15 + \tfrac{5}{4} = 15\tfrac{5}{4}$$

$$15\tfrac{5}{4} = 16\tfrac{1}{4}$$

$$5 * 3\tfrac{1}{4} = 16\tfrac{1}{4}$$

Check Your Understanding

Solve the following problems:

1. $1\tfrac{1}{2} \times 1\tfrac{1}{4}$ **2.** $2\tfrac{1}{3} \times 1\tfrac{2}{5}$ **3.** $3\tfrac{1}{6} * 1\tfrac{1}{3}$ **4.** $6 * 2\tfrac{1}{2}$

5. $3\tfrac{1}{5} \times 8$ **6.** $12 \times 4\tfrac{3}{4}$ **7.** $2\tfrac{1}{8} * 2\tfrac{1}{2}$ **8.** $3\tfrac{5}{6} * 2\tfrac{3}{4}$

Write your answers on a separate sheet of paper.

Partial-Quotients Algorithm for Division

*In the partial-quotients method, it takes several steps to find the quotient. At each step, you find a partial answer (called a **partial quotient**); then you find the product of the partial quotient and divisor and subtract it from the dividend. Finally, you add all the partial quotients to find the final quotient.*

Even those students whose basic-facts knowledge and estimation skills are limited can find correct answers using this commonsense approach. In the process, students quickly discover that the better their estimates, the fewer the steps.

Build Understanding

Using page 67, explain that with this method of dividing, students will be making mental estimates. Students may find it helpful to make a list of multiplication facts for the divisor. Use questions like the following to guide students through the example:

- When you make the first estimate, what question must you ask yourself? *(How many 6s are in 354?)*

- Why is a multiple of 10 a good number to start with? *(because multiples of 10 are easy numbers to work with)*

- Where do you record your guesses (or partial quotients)? *(in a separate column to the right of the problem)*

- How do you find the final quotient (the answer) and where is it recorded? *(You find the sum of the partial quotients and record it below the column to the right of the problem.)*

Error Alert Watch for students who make the first estimate as if they were using the standard long-division algorithm—that is, looking at only the first two digits of the dividend. Remind students that when they're using this algorithm, they have to think about the whole number, not part of the number. So the first estimate will be an answer to the question, "How many equal groups of the divisor are in the *whole* dividend?"

Check Understanding

Have a volunteer go to the board and solve a division problem. Encourage the student to explain her or his strategy while working so that the class can follow along. Have students direct their questions to the volunteer, and guide that student in answering as necessary. If many students are confused about a particular aspect of the algorithm, do another problem on the board. When you are reasonably certain that most of your students understand the algorithm, assign the "Check Your Understanding" exercises at the bottom of page 67. For more difficult problems, refer students to pages 68 and 69. *(See answers in margin.)*

Partial-Quotients Algorithm for Division (1-digit divisor)

To find the number of 6s in 354, first find all the partial quotients.
Record them in a column to the right of the problem. Then add
the partial quotients to find the final quotient or answer.

Example

(dividend) (divisor)
$$354 \div 6$$

Ask: How many [6s] are in 354? *(At least 50)*
The first partial quotient is 50.
50 * 6 = 300
Subtract 300 from 354.

```
6)354
  300  | 50
   54
   54  | 9
    0    59
```

Ask: How many [6s] are in 54? *(9)*
The second partial quotient is 9.
9 * 6 = 54
Subtract 54 from 54.

The difference is 0, so there is no remainder.

Add the partial quotients. The answer is 59.

$$354 \div 6 = 59$$

Check Your Understanding

Solve the following problems:

1. 135 ÷ 5   **2.** 736 ÷ 8   **3.** 292 ÷ 4

4. 6,730 ÷ 2   **5.** 392 ÷ 7   **6.** 204 ÷ 3

7. 9)171   **8.** 6)894

Partial-Quotients Algorithm for Division (2-digit divisor)

To find the number of 27s in 621, first find all the partial quotients. Record them in a column to the right of the problem. Then add the partial quotients to find the final quotient or answer.

Example

(dividend)   (divisor)

$$621 \div 27$$

Ask: How many [27s] are in 621? (*At least 20*)
The first partial quotient is 20.
20 * 27 = 540
Subtract 540 from 621.

```
27)621
   540  20
    81
    81   3
     0  23
```

Ask: How many [27s] are in 81? (*3*)
The second partial quotient is 3.
3 * 27 = 81
Subtract 81 from 81.

The difference is 0, so there is no remainder.

Add the partial quotients. The answer is 23.

$$621 \div 27 = 23$$

Check Your Understanding

Solve the following problems:

1. 273 ÷ 13   **2.** 342 ÷ 19   **3.** 768 ÷ 32

4. 902 ÷ 22   **5.** 425 ÷ 17   **6.** 630 ÷ 42

7. 36)828   **8.** 57)3,420

Partial-Quotients Algorithm for Division (2-digit divisor)

To find the number of 12s in 238, first find all the partial quotients. Record them in a column to the right of the problem. Then add the partial quotients to find the final quotient or answer.

Example

(dividend)   (divisor)
238 ÷ 12

Ask: How many [12s] are in 238? (*At least 10*)
The first partial quotient is 10.
10 * 12 = 120
Subtract 120 from 238.

Ask: How many [12s] are in 118? (*9*)
The second partial quotient is 9.
9 * 12 = 108
Subtract 108 from 118.
The difference is the remainder.

Add the partial quotients to find the quotient.
The answer is 19 R10.

```
12)238
    120 |10
    118
    108 | 9
     10  19
     ↑    ↑
Remainder  Quotient
```

238 ÷ 12 → 19 R10

Check Your Understanding

Solve the following problems:

1. 380 ÷ 20

2. 720 ÷ 40

3. 663 / 51

4. 972 ÷ 36

5. 841 / 52

6. 64)772

7. 895 ÷ 81

8. 94)6,392

Write your answers on a separate sheet of paper.

Column-Division Algorithm for Division

This algorithm for division connects a manipulative-based approach to paper-and-pencil. Making this connection allows students to conceptually understand the division process as they move to the symbolic level. This process encourages students to utilize base-10 blocks and language that breaks the dividend into separate digits. For example, 583 would focus on 5 things, 8 things, and 3 things rather than 583 items. The student breaks each part into hundreds, tens, and ones, with only one place value being considered at a time.

Even those students whose basic-facts knowledge and estimation skills are limited can find correct answers using this approach to division. In the process, students can move from the concrete to the paper-and-pencil level once they feel comfortable. This graphic column presentation greatly reduces error.

Build Understanding

Divide the class into groups of three. Provide each group with base-10 blocks and direct them to model the number 53 (5 tens, 3 ones). Tell students that the blocks represent 53 pieces of candy and direct them to divide the pieces equally among two students. When dividing the 5 longs among 2 students, the groups should see that they have to exchange one long for ten ones. The groups should determine that each student would receive 26 pieces of candy with 1 left over.

The sharing of base-10 blocks at each place value is the conceptual basis for this division algorithm. Explain that it is best to always begin with the largest base-10 blocks. If they can't be shared evenly, they should be exchanged for smaller base-10 blocks, as in the example above.

Using page 71, walk students through an example of the column-division algorithm.

Error Alert Watch for students who do not trade in one of the longs for 10 ones when dividing 53 into 2 groups. Do another example with these students to make sure they understand the process of equal grouping.

Check Understanding

Give each group 2 or 3 additional problems to solve. Encourage each student to explain his or her strategy while working so that the small group can follow along. If many students are confused about a particular aspect of the algorithm, do another problem as a whole class. When you are reasonably certain that most of your students understand the algorithm, assign the "Check Your Understanding" exercises at the bottom of page 71. *(See answers in margin.)*

Page 71
Answer Key

1. 151 R2

2. 121

3. 76

4. 66 R3

5. 208

6. 1,975 R1

7. 1,340 R3

8. 537 R11

Column-Division Algorithm for Division

In the example below, think of sharing $583 among 4 people.

1. Draw lines to separate the digits in the dividend. Work left to right. Begin in the left column.

$$4\overline{)\,5\ \vert\ 8\ \vert\ 3}$$

2. Think of the 5 in the hundreds column as 5 $100 bills to be shared by 4 people. Each person gets 1 $100 bill. There is 1 $100 bill remaining.

$$
\begin{array}{c}
1 \\
4\overline{)\,5\ \vert\ 8\ \vert\ 3} \\
-4 \\
\hline
1
\end{array}
$$

3. Trade the 1 $100 bill for 10 $10 bills. Think of the 8 in the tens column as 8 $10 bills. That makes 10 + 8 $10 bills in all.

$$
\begin{array}{c}
1 \\
4\overline{)\,5\ \vert\ 8\ \vert\ 3} \\
-4\ \vert\ 18 \\
\hline
1
\end{array}
$$

4. If 4 people share 18 $10 bills, each person gets 4 $10 bills. There are 2 $10 bills remaining.

$$
\begin{array}{cc}
1 & 4 \\
4\overline{)\,5} & 8\ \vert\ 3 \\
-4 & 18 \\
1 & -16 \\
\hline
 & 2
\end{array}
$$

5. Trade the 2 $10 bills for 20 $1 bills. Think of the 3 in the ones column as 3 $1 bills. That makes 20 + 3 = 23 $1 bills.

$$
\begin{array}{ccc}
1 & 4 & \\
4\overline{)\,5} & 8 & 3 \\
-4 & 18 & 23 \\
1 & -16 & \\
\hline
 & 2 &
\end{array}
$$

6. If 4 people share 23 $1 bills, each person gets 5 $1 bills. There are 3 $1 bills remaining.

Record the answer as 145 R3.
Each person receives $145 and $3 are left over.

$$
\begin{array}{ccc}
1 & 4 & 5 \\
4\overline{)\,5} & 8 & 3 \\
-4 & 18 & 23 \\
1 & -16 & -20 \\
\hline
 & 2 & 3
\end{array}
$$

Check Your Understanding

Solve the following problems:

1. 455 ÷ 3 **2.** 726 ÷ 6 **3.** 532 / 7 **4.** 267 / 4

5. 832 / 4 **6.** 3,951 ÷ 2 **7.** 6,703 / 5 **8.** 8,603 / 16

Write your answers on a separate sheet of paper.

Long Algorithm (Standard) for Division (with Models)

The long algorithm (standard) for division is the one that is familiar to most adults and many children. The person using this algorithm places the dividend within a division bracket and the divisor outside and to the left of the bracket. The problem solver then makes a series of educated multiplication/division estimates, records the result of each estimate underneath the dividend, and subtracts the result of each estimate from the number above it. If there is a remainder, the problem solver writes it next to the quotient.

The traditional method for teaching this algorithm is to begin with models (such as base-10 blocks), using them to demonstrate the process of dividing a dividend into equal groups.

Build Understanding

Divide the class into groups of four or five, provide each group with base-10 blocks, and direct each group to model the number 138 using the least number of blocks. When each group has built the correct model (consisting of 1 hundred, 3 tens, and 8 ones), ask students to divide the model into 6 equal groups. Allow each group to tackle the problem in its own way. If students seem confused about how to start, however, suggest that they think about regrouping or trading the largest block (the hundred) for 10 tens. Continue guiding students as necessary until each group of students has successfully changed 1 hundred, 3 tens, and 8 ones into six equal groupings of 2 tens and 3 ones each.

Using page 73, explain that with this method of dividing, students will begin by making an estimate about what the first digit in the quotient (the answer) should be. Use questions like the following to guide students through the example:

- Why do you have to trade 3 hundreds for 30 tens? *(because 3 hundreds cannot be divided into 8 equal groups)*

- Why do you have to trade 1 ten for 10 ones? *(because 1 ten cannot be divided into 8 equal groups)*

- What does the last picture tell you? *(that 331 blocks are divided into 8 groups, 41 blocks in each group, and 3 blocks left over)*

Error Alert Watch for students who are multiplying incorrectly. Remind students that although the long-division process may seem complex, each multiplication step within the process is a simple, basic-fact step. Also, watch for students who are subtracting incorrectly. Suggest that these students cover the numbers above the numbers being subtracted with their index fingers to help them focus on only two numbers at a time—the two they are subtracting.

Check Understanding

Have students check each of their answers by multiplying the quotient by the divisor, adding the remainder if there is one, and then checking to see if the result matches the dividend. Have a volunteer go to the board and solve a division problem using the standard algorithm. Help the student describe the process while he or she works through it and correct any misconceptions as necessary, referring again to base-10 blocks or arrays if they seem to help. When you are reasonably certain that most of your students understand the algorithm, assign the "Check Your Understanding" exercises at the bottom of page 73. *(See answers in margin.)*

Page 73
Answer Key

1. 49

2. 63

3. 36

4. 82

5. 87

6. 83

7. 23 R7

8. 99 R3

Long Algorithm (Standard) for Division (with Models)

Use base-10 blocks to model the dividend. Then make trades until you have the correct number of equal groups.

Example

(dividend) (divisor)
331 ÷ 8

3 hundreds cannot be divided into 8 equal groups.

So rename 3 hundreds as 30 tens.

$8\overline{)331}$

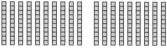

Divide 33 tens into 8 equal groups.

Each group has 4 tens, and 1 ten remains.

$$\begin{array}{r} 4 \\ 8\overline{)331} \\ \underline{32} \\ 1 \end{array}$$

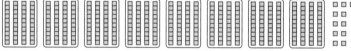

1 ten cannot be divided into 8 equal groups.

So rename 1 ten as 10 ones. There are now 11 ones.

$$\begin{array}{r} 4 \\ 8\overline{)331} \\ \underline{32} \\ 11 \end{array}$$

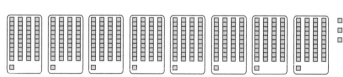

Divide 11 ones into 8 equal groups.

3 ones remain.

$$\begin{array}{r} 41 \\ 8\overline{)331} \\ \underline{32} \\ 11 \\ \underline{8} \\ 3 \end{array}$$

331 ÷ 8 → 41 R3

Check Your Understanding

Solve the following problems:

1. $5\overline{)245}$ **2.** 504 ÷ 8   **3.** 144 / 4   **4.** 574 ÷ 7

5. $3\overline{)261}$ **6.** $6\overline{)498}$ **7.** 214 / 9   **8.** 795 / 8

Write your answers on a separate sheet of paper.

Long Algorithm (Standard) for Division

The long algorithm (standard) for division is the one that is familiar to most adults and many children. The person using this algorithm places the dividend within a division bracket and the divisor outside and to the left of the bracket. The problem solver then makes a series of educated multiplication/division estimates, records the result of each estimate underneath the dividend, and subtracts the result of each estimate from the number above it. If there is a remainder, the problem solver writes it next to the quotient.

The traditional method for teaching this algorithm is to begin with models (such as base-10 blocks) and then gradually move toward the use of symbols (that is, numerals) only.

Build Understanding

Review the process of making division estimates. Give students such problems as $48 \div 9$; $77 \div 10$; $82 \div 8$; and $56 \div 6$. Remind students to use a basic fact as the basis for each estimate, and explain that it is acceptable to have a number left over. Then write the following problem on the board: $312 \div 6$. Have students estimate the first digit of the quotient, and remind them to use their basic-facts knowledge (their "fact power") to estimate how many 6s are in 31 *(5 with 1 left over)*. Then work through the entire problem together on the board $(312 \div 6 = 52)$. Finally, provide one more example—$574 \div 7$—and encourage students to exercise their mental-math skills when making estimates.

Note: Although the aim is to have students use mental math when estimating, allow those students who seem to be struggling with the process to write down their estimates, at least initially.

Using page 75, explain that with this method of dividing, students will begin by making an estimate about what the first digit in the quotient (the answer) should be. Use questions like the following to guide students through the example (and through other examples you provide):

- What will you multiply the divisor by to get a number as close to the first (two) digits as possible?

- How will you know if you have estimated correctly? *(Multiply the estimate by the divisor and then subtract the product from the first [two] digits. If the difference is greater than the divisor, then the estimate is too low—so try again!)*

Error Alert Watch for students who accept an estimate that is too low. If necessary, have students circle or highlight the divisor with a pen or pencil of another color to remind themselves to keep checking each remainder against the divisor.

Check Understanding

Divide students into pairs. Have one student in each pair solve a division problem orally, explaining each step as it is written on a sheet of paper. Have the person's partner listen and watch for errors and omissions. Then have partners exchange places and solve a second problem. When you are reasonably certain that most of your students understand the algorithm, assign the "Check Your Understanding" exercises at the bottom of page 75. *(See answers in margin.)*

Page 75 Answer Key

1. 43

2. 86

3. 99

4. 26

5. 85

6. 298

7. 571

8. 608 R2

Long Algorithm (Standard) for Division

Estimate to find the first digit of the quotient. Write that digit correctly above the dividend and multiply it by the divisor. Write the product below in the dividend. Find the difference and bring down the next number in the dividend. Repeat the procedure until you have used all the numbers in the dividend.

Example

$$3,843 \div 7$$

- **Think: How many 7s are in 38?** (5)
  Write 5 in the quotient, above the 8.
  Multiply 5×7. (35)
  Subtract 35 from 38. (3)
  Bring down the 4 from the dividend. (to make 34)

```
      549
7)3,843
   35
   34
   28
    63
    63
     0
```

- **Think: How many 7s are in 34?** (4)
  Write 4 next to 5 in the quotient.
  Multiply 4×7. (28)
  Subtract 28 from 34. (6)
  Bring down the 3 from the dividend. (to make 63)

- **Think: How many 7s are in 63?** (9)
  Write 9 next to 4 in the quotient.
  Multiply 9×7. (63)
  Subtract 63 from 63. (0)

$$3,843 \div 7 = 549$$

Check Your Understanding

Solve the following problems:

1. $172 \div 4$ **2.** $5\overline{)430}$ **3.** $2\overline{)198}$

4. $182 \div 7$ **5.** $9\overline{)765}$ **6.** $894 \div 3$

7. $4,568 / 8$ **8.** $3,042 \div 5$

Write your answers on a separate sheet of paper.   **Division Algorithms 75**

Column-Division Algorithm for Decimal Division

The column-division algorithm for division of whole numbers can easily be applied to the division of decimals. It looks just like the algorithm for whole numbers, except we are inserting decimals in the quotient at the end of the problem. When this algorithm is applied to decimals the student must first think of a power of 10 that, when multiplied by the divisor, will change the divisor into a whole number. Once both divisor and dividend have been adjusted by the same power of 10, division can take place as it does with whole numbers.

Build Understanding

If students need to review the whole-number version of this algorithm, refer them to page 71. Review multiplying decimals by powers of 10. Then give students numbers like 0.5, 0.03, and 0.0008, and ask them by what power of 10 they would multiply each number to make it a whole number.

Using page 77, tell students to begin multiplying both the divisor and the dividend by the power of 10 that makes the divisor a whole number. Explain to students that this process creates an equivalent problem. Fractional equivalents might help students see that this is true–0.324 / 0.04 (multiplied by 10) = 3.24 / 0.4 (multiplied by 10) = 32.4 / 4. Use questions like the following to guide students through the example:

- By which power of 10 would you multiply 0.04 to make it a whole number? *(100)*

- Which number do you place to the left of the division bracket? *(4)*

- Will you need to make any trades before you share? *(yes, trade 3 tens for 30 ones)*

- Where do you place the decimal point in your answer? *(above the decimal point in the dividend; 8.1)*

Error Alert Watch for students who multiply the divisor and the dividend by different powers of 10. Make sure that students select the power of 10 based on the divisor and that they multiply both the divisor and the dividend by that power of 10.

Check Understanding

Have a volunteer go to the board and model the column algorithm for decimal division for the problem 6.74 ÷ 0.5. Encourage the student to explain what he or she is doing while working so that the class can follow along. Have students direct their questions to the volunteer, and guide that student in answering as necessary. If many students are confused about a particular aspect of the algorithm, do another problem on the board. When you are reasonably certain that most students understand the algorithm, assign the "Check Your Understanding" exercises at the bottom of page 77. Notice that Exercise 7 involves a 2-digit divisor. Exercise 8 requires students to insert a zero between the decimal point and the first digit in the quotient. *(See answers in margin.)*

**Page 77
Answer Key**

1. 120.1

2. 0.15

3. 0.87

4. 1,490

5. 61

6. 1.62

7. 21.5

8. 0.0182

Column-Division Algorithm for Decimal Division

Think of a power of 10 that will make the divisor a whole number. Multiply both the divisor and the dividend by the same power of ten. Then divide as you would for whole numbers. Remember to correctly place the decimal point in the quotient.

Example

(dividend)　(divisor)
0.324 ÷ 0.04

Decide which power of ten multiplied by the divisor will make the divisor a whole number.

$$0.324 * 100 = 32.4$$
$$0.04 * 100 = 4$$

Multiply both the divisor and the dividend by this power of 10.

Write the new problem.

$$4)\ 3\ |\ 2.\ |\ 4$$

Trade the 3 tens for 30 ones.
That makes 30 + 2 ones in all.
Record 32 in the ones column.

$$4)\ 3\ |\ 2.\ |\ 4$$
$$32$$

Place a decimal point in the quotient directly above the one in the dividend.

$$8.$$
$$4)\ 3\ |\ 2.\ |\ 4$$
$$32$$
$$-\ 32$$

There are 8[4s] in 32. **Record** this in the answer space. 8 * 4 = 32.
Record 32 in the ones column. Subtract.

There is 1[4] in 4. **Record** this in the answer space. 1 * 4 = 4.
Record 4 in the tenths column. Subtract.

$$8.\ |\ 1$$
$$4)\ 3\ |\ 2.\ |\ 4$$
$$32\ |\ -\ 4$$
$$-\ 32\ |\ 0$$
$$0\ |$$

0.324 ÷ 0.04 = 8.1

Check Your Understanding

Solve the following problems:

1. 36.03 ÷ 0.3　　**2.** 0.0075 ÷ 0.05　**3.** 0.0261 / 0.03　　**4.** 0.006)8.94

5. 2.44 / 0.04　　**6.** 0.0486 ÷ 0.03　**7.** 40.85 / 1.9　　**8.** 0.3)0.00546

Write your answers on a separate sheet of paper.

Long Algorithm (Standard) for Decimal Division

The long division algorithm (standard) is the one that is familiar to most adults and many children. When applied to decimals, the problem solver must first think of a power of 10 that, when multiplied by the divisor, will change the divisor into a whole number. Once both divisor and dividend have been adjusted by the same power of 10, division can take place as it does with whole numbers.

Build Understanding

If students need to review the whole-number version of this algorithm, refer them to page 75.

Review multiplying decimals by powers of 10. Then give students numbers like 0.3, 0.09, and 0.006, and ask them by what power of 10 they would multiply each number to make it a whole number.

Using page 79, tell students to begin by multiplying both the divisor and the dividend by the power of 10 that makes the divisor a whole number. Explain to students that this process creates an equivalent problem. Fractional equivalents might help students see that this is true — 0.216 / 0.06 = 2.16 / 0.6 = 21.6 / 6. Use questions like the following to guide students through the example:

- By which power of 10 would you multiply 0.06 to make it a whole number? *(100)*

- Which number do you place to the left of the division bracket? *(6)*

- Which division fact can help you estimate the first digit of the quotient? *(18 ÷ 6 = 3)*

- Where do you place the decimal point in your answer? *(above the decimal point in the dividend; 21.6)*

Error Alert Watch for students who multiply the divisor and dividend by different powers of 10. Make sure that students select the power of 10 based on the *divisor* and that they then multiply *both* the divisor and the dividend by that power of 10.

Check Understanding

Have a volunteer go to the board and model the long (standard) division algorithm for the problem 36.5 ÷ 0.5. Encourage the student to explain what he or she is doing while working so that the class can follow along. Have students direct their questions to the volunteer, and guide that student in answering as necessary. If many students are confused about a particular aspect of the algorithm, do another problem on the board. When you are reasonably certain that most of your students understand the algorithm, assign the "Check Your Understanding" exercises at the bottom of page 79. Notice that Exercise 8 requires students to insert a zero between the decimal point and the first digit in the quotient. *(See answers in margin.)*

Long Algorithm (Standard) for Decimal Division

Think of a power of 10 that will make the divisor a whole number. Multiply both the divisor and dividend by the same power of 10.

Then divide as you would with whole numbers. Remember to correctly place the decimal point in the quotient.

(dividend)   (divisor)

Example $0.216 \div 0.06$

Decide which power of 10 multiplied by the divisor will make the divisor a whole number.

$0.06 * 100 = 6$

Multiply both the divisor and the dividend by this power of 10.

$0.216 * 100 = 21.6$

Write the result as a division problem with a division bracket.

Divide as you would with whole numbers.

Place a decimal point in the quotient directly above the one in the dividend.

$$\begin{array}{r} 3.6 \\ 6\overline{)21.6} \\ 18 \\ \hline 36 \\ 36 \\ \hline 0 \end{array}$$

$$0.216 \div 0.06 = 3.6$$

Check Your Understanding

Solve the following problems:

1. $0.108 \div 0.04$ **2.** $5.74 / 0.7$ **3.** $0.9\overline{)17.1}$

4. $0.03\overline{)0.0261}$ **5.** $0.075 / 0.005$ **6.** $4.72 \div 0.8$

7. $0.474 / 0.6$ **8.** $0.02496 \div 0.4$

Write your answers on a separate sheet of paper.

Converting Common Fractions to Decimals

In order to convert common fractions to decimals students use a procedure that requires dividing the numerator of the fraction by the denominator. Students of Everyday Mathematics have solved division problems written as fractions since fourth grade. The numerator is the dividend of the problem and the denominator is the divisor of the problem. Some fractions require adding a decimal point and one or more zeros to the dividend in order to carry out the division process.

Build Understanding

Review the process of making division estimates. Give students such problems as $45 \div 8 =$, $88 \div 10 =$, and so on. Remind students to use a basic fact as the basis for the estimate. Then write $\frac{1}{4}$ on the board. Explain to students that this fraction can be written as a division problem. Rewrite this fraction writing the dividend (1) within a division bracket and the divisor (4) outside to the left of the bracket. Place a decimal point to the right of the dividend, and attach two zeros after the last digit of the dividend. Then work through the entire problem together on the board. $1 \div 4 = 0.25$, or $\frac{1}{4} = 0.25$.

Using page 81, explain how to convert the common fraction $\frac{1}{6}$ to a decimal. Use questions like the following to guide students through this procedure.

- How do I rewrite this problem using the division bracket?

- Why do we attach zeros to the dividend?

- How many zeros did you need to attach for this problem?

Error Alert Watch for students who attach zeros and place the decimal incorrectly. Also look for students who switch around the divisor (denominator) and dividend (numerator) when writing the problem with the division bracket. Watch to make sure students drop down the zeros as needed.

Check Understanding

Select a volunteer to come up to the board to work through another problem. While the student records on the board encourage the class to follow along with their own recordings. Students should ask the volunteer questions if they do not understand the procedure. Work through additional examples as needed. When you are reasonably certain that most students understand the procedure, assign the "Check Your Understanding" exercises at the bottom of page 81. *(See answers in margin.)*

Page 81
Answer Key

1. 0.75

2. 0.8

3. 0.875

4. $0.\overline{3}$

5. 0.4

6. 0.625

7. $0.\overline{4}$

8. $0.\overline{714285}$

Converting Common Fractions to Decimals

Write the fraction as a division problem using the division bracket. (Write the numerator as the dividend and the denominator as the divisor.) Place a decimal point after the dividend and attach zeros. Work through the division process, recording the quotient above the dividend.

Example Convert to a decimal. $\dfrac{1}{6}$

Write the fraction using the division bracket. Place a decimal after the dividend and attach two zeros.

$$6\overline{)1.00}$$

How many 6s are in 10? Record the answer in the tenths place. Bring down the next zero.

$$\begin{array}{r} .16 \\ 6\overline{)1.000} \\ 6 \\ \hline 40 \\ 36 \\ \hline 4 \end{array}$$

How many 6s are in 40? Record the answer in the hundredths place. Since there is still a remainder, attach one more zero to the dividend. Bring down the zero.

Continue to divide until you see a pattern. (The 6 will continue to repeat in the quotient.)

$$\begin{array}{r} .166 = .1\overline{6} \\ 6\overline{)1.000} \\ 6 \\ \hline 40 \\ 36 \\ \hline 40 \\ 36 \\ \hline 4 \end{array}$$

This type of common fraction converts into a repeating decimal. Write this by placing a bar over the first 6 to indicate it will repeat.

$$\dfrac{1}{6} = .1\overline{6}$$

Check Your Understanding

Convert the following common fractions to decimals:

1. $\dfrac{3}{4}$ **2.** $\dfrac{4}{5}$ **3.** $\dfrac{7}{8}$

4. $\dfrac{1}{3}$ **5.** $\dfrac{2}{5}$ **6.** $\dfrac{5}{8}$

7. $\dfrac{4}{9}$ **8.** $\dfrac{5}{7}$

Write your answers on a separate sheet of paper.

Fraction Division (with Models)

Consider a typical whole-number division problem like 41 ÷ 3. People often solve it by thinking about how many 3s are in 41. The same thought process applies to the division of fractions, and when used in combination with fraction models, helps students gain meaningful understanding of dividing fractions.

Build Understanding

Have students use graph paper or templates to draw fraction models. As a review, ask students to represent fractions like $\frac{1}{2}$, $\frac{1}{3}$, $\frac{1}{6}$, and $\frac{2}{3}$. Encourage students to use a variety of shapes, such as squares, circles, hexagons, and triangles. Ask students how they would represent a whole number, such as 5.

Using page 83, explain that students will use models to show the division. In Example 1, thinking about pizzas can help students visualize how many $\frac{1}{3}$s are in 5. If you have 5 pizzas, and divide each pizza into $\frac{1}{3}$s, then you have 15 portions. In Example 2, if you have $\frac{1}{2}$ of a pizza and want portions in $\frac{1}{6}$s, you divide the whole pizza into portions, each one the size of $\frac{1}{6}$ of a pizza. You end up with 3 portions. Use questions like the following to guide students through the examples:

- How do you represent the dividend? (*Draw the number of shapes needed—whole shapes for whole numbers and a part of a shape for any fraction less than 1.*)

- How would you divide each unit? (*Divide each unit into the number of equal pieces identified by the divisor.*)

- How do you find the quotient? (*Count the total number of pieces.*)

Error Alert Watch for students with inaccurate drawings, especially when both the dividend and the divisor are fractions. Remind students that they need to divide each *whole unit shape* into the number of equal pieces identified by the divisor.

Check Understanding

Have students work in pairs, and instruct partners to take turns drawing models. Circulate around the room checking drawings. Then work through a couple of additional examples if necessary. When you are reasonably certain that most of your students understand the algorithm, assign the "Check Your Understanding" exercises at the bottom of page 83. (*See answers in margin.*)

Page 83 Answer Key

1. 8

2. 4

3. 2

4. 2

5. 12

6. 16

7. 4

8. $\frac{2}{3}$

Fraction Division (with Models)

Draw a picture or pictures to show the dividend. Then draw lines to show division of each unit by the divisor. Count the parts to find the quotient.

(dividend)   (divisor)
$$5 \div \frac{1}{3}$$

Example 1

Show 5.

Draw lines or trade pieces to show the division of each unit by $\frac{1}{3}$.

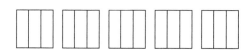

There are 15 $\frac{1}{3}$ s in 5.

$$5 \div \frac{1}{3} = 15$$

$$\frac{1}{2} \div \frac{1}{6}$$

Example 2

Show $\frac{1}{2}$.

Draw lines or trade pieces to show the division of the whole unit by $\frac{1}{6}$.

There are 3 $\frac{1}{6}$ s in $\frac{1}{2}$.

$$\frac{1}{2} \div \frac{1}{6} = 3$$

Check Your Understanding

Solve the following problems:

1. $4 \div \frac{1}{2}$

2. $\frac{1}{2} \div \frac{1}{8}$

3. $\frac{1}{3} \div \frac{1}{6}$

4. $\frac{1}{5} \div \frac{1}{10}$

5. $3 \div \frac{1}{4}$

6. $2 \div \frac{1}{8}$

7. $\frac{2}{3} \div \frac{1}{6}$

8. $\frac{1}{3} \div \frac{1}{2}$

Write your answers on a separate sheet of paper.

Fraction Division

To divide two fractions, problem solvers multiply the first fraction by the reciprocal of the second fraction. In Everyday Mathematics, *this is called the Division of Fractions Property, and it is based on several mathematical rules regarding fractions and the reciprocal relationship between multiplication and division.*

Build Understanding

Review finding reciprocals. Remind students that they need to rename whole numbers and mixed numbers as fractions before they can find their reciprocals. Ask students to find the reciprocal of $\frac{1}{3}$ (3), 7 ($\frac{1}{7}$), $2\frac{2}{3}$ ($\frac{3}{8}$), and $\frac{5}{6}$ ($\frac{6}{5}$, *or* $1\frac{1}{5}$).

Using the example $\frac{1}{6} \div \frac{3}{2}$, walk students through the steps below so that they understand why the Division of Fractions Property works.

- Multiply the first fraction by the reciprocal of the second fraction.

$$\frac{1}{6} \div \frac{3}{2} = \frac{1}{6} \times \frac{2}{3}$$

- Simplify as needed.

$$= \frac{2}{18}, \text{ or } \frac{1}{9}$$

Use the example $2\frac{3}{4} \div 11$ to explain the division of mixed numbers.

- Change any whole number or mixed number to an improper fraction.

$$2\frac{3}{4} \div 11 = \frac{11}{4} \div \frac{11}{1}$$

- Multiply the first fraction by the reciprocal of the second fraction.

$$= \frac{11}{4} \times \frac{1}{11}$$

- Simplify as needed.

$$= \frac{11}{44} = \frac{1}{4}$$

Error Alert Watch for students who use incorrect reciprocals or just change the problem from division to multiplication without using reciprocals. You may want to have students write and label the reciprocal of each divisor before they begin each problem.

Check Understanding

Divide the class into groups of 3 or 4 and assign a leader in each group to explain the steps in the examples. Tell group members to direct their questions to their group leader. When you are reasonably certain that most of your students understand the algorithm, assign the "Check Your Understanding" exercises at the bottom of page 85. *(See answers in margin.)*

Page 85
Answer Key

1. $\frac{2}{3}$

2. $\frac{1}{6}$

3. 16

4. $\frac{1}{6}$

5. $\frac{2}{9}$

6. 6

7. 15

8. $1\frac{1}{2}$

Fraction Division

Use the Division of Fractions Property to divide. That is, to find the quotient of two fractions, multiply the first fraction by the reciprocal of the second fraction.

> **Division of Fractions Property**
>
> $$\frac{a}{b} \div \frac{c}{d} = \frac{a}{b} * \frac{d}{c}$$

Example 1

$$\frac{4}{5} \div \frac{2}{3} =$$

Multiply the first fraction by the reciprocal of the second fraction.

$$\frac{4}{5} * \frac{3}{2} = \frac{12}{10} = 1\frac{2}{10}, \text{ or } 1\frac{1}{5}$$

Simplify as needed.

Example 2

$$4 \div 1\frac{1}{3}$$

Rename whole numbers or mixed numbers as improper fractions.

$$\frac{4}{1} \div \frac{4}{3}$$

Multiply the first fraction by the reciprocal of the second fraction.

$$\frac{4}{1} * \frac{3}{4} = 3$$

Check Your Understanding

Solve the following problems:

1. $\frac{1}{3} \div \frac{1}{2}$

2. $\frac{2}{3} \div 4$

3. $6 \div \frac{3}{8}$

4. $\frac{1}{8} \div \frac{3}{4}$

5. $\frac{1}{6} \div \frac{3}{4}$

6. $4 \div \frac{2}{3}$

7. $9 \div \frac{3}{5}$

8. $1\frac{7}{8} \div 1\frac{1}{4}$

Write your answers on a separate sheet of paper.

Answers to Practice Set 1A

While these problems may be appropriate for third grade students, feel free to assign some or all of them to any student who needs practice at this level.

This Practice Set emphasizes addition, subtraction, mulitplication, and division of whole numbers.

Name _____   Date _____   Time _____

Practice Set 1A

Use your favorite strategies to solve the following problems:

1. 8 + 6 14

2. 9 + 7 16

3. 27 − 4 23

4. 32 − 2 30

5. 5 × 9 45

6. 4 × 4 16

7. 30 × 7 210

8. 20 × 5 100

9. 16 ÷ 8 2

10. 63 ÷ 7 9

11. 52 ÷ 2 26

12. 39 ÷ 3 13

13.
```
   71
 + 10
   81
```

14.
```
   15
 ×  4
   60
```

15.
```
   22
4)88
```

16.
```
  109
 + 37
  146
```

17.
```
  158
 + 14
  172
```

18.
```
   15
6)90
```

19.
```
  167
 − 19
  148
```

20.
```
   11
10)110
```

21.
```
   15
8)120
```

22.
```
  294
 + 357
  651
```

23.
```
  308
 − 289
   19
```

24.
```
  500
 − 291
  209
```

25. Tamara has 23 barrettes and headbands in all. She has 9 headbands. How many barrettes does she have? __14 barrettes__

26. 36 third graders are going on a field trip. If they sit 3 to a row on the bus, how many rows will they fill? __12 rows__

27. A chart in the classroom has 30 little boxes going down and 9 little boxes going across. How many little boxes are on the chart? __270 little boxes__

Write your answers on a separate sheet of paper.

Practice Sets 87

Practice Set 1A

Use your favorite strategies to solve the following problems:

1. 8 + 6

2. 9 + 7

3. 27 − 4

4. 32 − 2

5. 5 × 9

6. 4 × 4

7. 30 × 7

8. 20 × 5

9. 16 ÷ 8

10. 63 ÷ 7

11. 52 ÷ 2

12. 39 ÷ 3

13.   71
  + 10

14.   15
  × 4

15. 4)88

16.   109
  + 37

17.   158
  + 14

18. 6)90

19.   167
  − 19

20. 10)110

21. 8)120

22.   294
  + 357

23.   308
  − 289

24.   500
  − 291

25. Tamara has 23 barrettes and headbands in all. She has 9 headbands. How many barrettes does she have? _____

26. 36 third graders are going on a field trip. If they sit 3 to a row on the bus, how many rows will they fill? _____

27. A chart in the classroom has 30 little boxes going down and 9 little boxes going across. How many little boxes are on the chart? _____

Answers to Practice Set 1B

While these problems may be appropriate for third grade students, feel free to assign some or all of them to any student who needs practice at this level.

This Practice Set emphasizes addition, subtraction, mulitplication, and division of whole numbers.

Name   Date   Time

Practice Set 1B

Use your favorite strategies to solve the following problems:

1. 7 + 5 12   **2.** 8 + 4 12   **3.** 25 − 4 21

4. 18 − 5 13   **5.** 6 × 7 42   **6.** 8 × 5 40

7. 20 × 6 120   **8.** 50 × 5 250   **9.** 15 ÷ 5 3

10. 45 ÷ 9 5   **11.** 27 ÷ 3 9   **12.** 36 ÷ 6 6

13.   82   **14.**   15   **15.** $5\overline{)65}$ → 13
        + 6   × 3
         88   45

16. 132   **17.** 105   **18.** $3\overline{)240}$ → 80
        + 17   + 22
         149   127

19. 139   **20.** $10\overline{)130}$ 13   **21.** $7\overline{)140}$ → 20
        − 17
         122

22. 129   **23.** 452   **24.** 400
        + 413   − 225   − 221
         542   227   179

25. Sam has 32 baseball and basketball trading cards. He has 15 baseball cards. How many basketball cards does he have? __17 basketball cards__

26. There are 20 cookies. There are 5 children. Each child will get the same number of cookies. How many cookies will each child get? ___4 cookies___

27. A piece of graph paper has 20 little boxes going down the paper and 10 little boxes going across. How many little boxes are on the graph paper? __200 little boxes__

Write your answers on a separate sheet of paper.   **Practice Sets   89**

Practice Set 1B

Use your favorite strategies to solve the following problems:

1. 7 + 5

2. 8 + 4

3. 25 − 4

4. 18 − 5

5. 6 × 7

6. 8 × 5

7. 20 × 6

8. 50 × 5

9. 15 ÷ 5

10. 45 ÷ 9

11. 27 ÷ 3

12. 36 ÷ 6

13.   82
     + 6

14.   15
     × 3

15. 5)$\overline{65}$

16.   132
     + 17

17.   105
     + 22

18. 3)$\overline{240}$

19.   139
     − 17

20. 10)$\overline{130}$

21. 7)$\overline{140}$

22.   129
     + 413

23.   452
     − 225

24.   400
     − 221

25. Sam has 32 baseball and basketball trading cards. He has 15 baseball cards. How many basketball cards does he have? _____

26. There are 20 cookies. There are 5 children. Each child will get the same number of cookies. How many cookies will each child get? _____

27. A piece of graph paper has 20 little boxes going down the paper and 10 little boxes going across. How many little boxes are on the graph paper? _____

Write your answers on a separate sheet of paper.

Answers to Practice Set 2A

While these problems may be appropriate for third grade students, feel free to assign some or all of them to any student who needs practice at this level.

This Practice Set emphasizes addition, subtraction, mulitplication, and division of whole numbers. Note the use of two different multiplication symbols (× and *).

Name _____ Date _____ Time _____

Practice Set 2A

Use your favorite strategies to solve the following problems:

1. 43 + 61 104   **2.** 85 − 14 71   **3.** 12 × 6 72

4. 17 × 9 153   **5.** 19 * 5 95   **6.** 463 + 159 622

7. 701 − 366 335   **8.** 316 ÷ 2 158   **9.** 408 − 350 58

10. 21 * 7 147   **11.** 18 * 3 54   **12.** 688 ÷ 8 86

13. 32
     × 4
     128

14. 969
     + 238
     1,207

15. $\overset{64}{7\overline{)448}}$

16. 190
     × 5
     950

17. 386
     − 169
     217

18. $\overset{35}{4\overline{)140}}$

19. 737
     + 428
     1,165

20. 463
     × 5
     2,315

21. 427
     − 263
     164

22. 878
     − 391
     487

23. 6,000
     × 9
     54,000

24. 575
     × 5
     2,875

25. Theo had 75 cents. He spent 21 cents. How much money does he have now? __54 cents__

26. In the store, there are 5 rows of oranges with 12 oranges in each row. How many oranges are in the store? __60 oranges__

27. Rashan has 42 puppy stickers and 56 kitten stickers. How many stickers does she have in all? __98 stickers__

Write your answers on a separate sheet of paper.

Practice Sets 91

Practice Set 2A

Use your favorite strategies to solve the following problems:

1. 43 + 61

2. 85 − 14

3. 12 × 6

4. 17 × 9

5. 19 * 5

6. 463 + 159

7. 701 − 366

8. 316 ÷ 2

9. 408 − 350

10. 21 * 7

11. 18 * 3

12. 688 ÷ 8

13.
$$\begin{array}{r} 32 \\ \times\ 4 \\ \hline \end{array}$$

14.
$$\begin{array}{r} 969 \\ +\ 238 \\ \hline \end{array}$$

15. $7\overline{)448}$

16.
$$\begin{array}{r} 190 \\ \times\ 5 \\ \hline \end{array}$$

17.
$$\begin{array}{r} 386 \\ -\ 169 \\ \hline \end{array}$$

18. $4\overline{)140}$

19.
$$\begin{array}{r} 737 \\ +\ 428 \\ \hline \end{array}$$

20.
$$\begin{array}{r} 463 \\ \times\ 5 \\ \hline \end{array}$$

21.
$$\begin{array}{r} 427 \\ -\ 263 \\ \hline \end{array}$$

22.
$$\begin{array}{r} 878 \\ -\ 391 \\ \hline \end{array}$$

23.
$$\begin{array}{r} 6,000 \\ \times\ 9 \\ \hline \end{array}$$

24.
$$\begin{array}{r} 575 \\ \times\ 5 \\ \hline \end{array}$$

25. Theo had 75 cents. He spent 21 cents. How much money does he have now? _____

26. In the store, there are 5 rows of oranges with 12 oranges in each row. How many oranges are in the store? _____

27. Rashan has 42 puppy stickers and 56 kitten stickers. How many stickers does she have in all? _____

Answers to Practice Set 2B

While these problems may be appropriate for third grade students, feel free to assign some or all of them to any student who needs practice at this level.

This Practice Set emphasizes addition, subtraction, mulitplication, and division of whole numbers. Note the use of two different multiplication symbols (× and *).

Name _____ Date _____ Time _____

Practice Set 2B

Use your favorite strategies to solve the following problems:

1. 54 + 62 116   **2.** 76 – 63 13   **3.** 11 × 4 44

4. 15 × 6 90   **5.** 14 * 7 98   **6.** 587 + 144 731

7. 603 – 234 369   **8.** 216 ÷ 4 54   **9.** 509 – 270 239

10. 31 * 8 248   **11.** 15 * 4 60   **12.** 725 ÷ 5 145

13. $\begin{array}{r} 43 \\ \times\ 6 \\ \hline 258 \end{array}$ **14.** $\begin{array}{r} 858 \\ +\ 325 \\ \hline 1{,}183 \end{array}$ **15.** $\begin{array}{r} 132 \\ 6\overline{)792} \end{array}$

16. $\begin{array}{r} 280 \\ \times\ \ 8 \\ \hline 2{,}240 \end{array}$ **17.** $\begin{array}{r} 378 \\ -\ 159 \\ \hline 219 \end{array}$ **18.** $\begin{array}{r} 20 \\ 8\overline{)160} \end{array}$

19. $\begin{array}{r} 686 \\ +\ 528 \\ \hline 1{,}214 \end{array}$ **20.** $\begin{array}{r} 346 \\ \times\ \ 5 \\ \hline 1{,}730 \end{array}$ **21.** $\begin{array}{r} 572 \\ -\ 326 \\ \hline 246 \end{array}$

22. $\begin{array}{r} 595 \\ -\ 271 \\ \hline 324 \end{array}$ **23.** $\begin{array}{r} 8{,}000 \\ \times\ \ \ 8 \\ \hline 64{,}000 \end{array}$ **24.** $\begin{array}{r} 464 \\ \times\ \ 4 \\ \hline 1{,}856 \end{array}$

25. Thomas has 52 cents. The candy he wants is 75 cents. How much more money does Thomas need to buy the candy? _____ 23 cents _____

26. In the parking lot, there are 3 rows of cars, with 15 cars in each row. How many cars are there in the parking lot? _____ 45 cars _____

27. Silvana has 8 roses and 17 carnations. How many flowers does she have in all? _____ 25 flowers _____

Write your answers on a separate sheet of paper.   **Practice Sets 93**

Practice Set 2B

Use your favorite strategies to solve the following problems:

1. 54 + 62

2. 76 − 63

3. 11 × 4

4. 15 × 6

5. 14 * 7

6. 587 + 144

7. 603 − 234

8. 216 ÷ 4

9. 509 − 270

10. 31 * 8

11. 15 * 4

12. 725 ÷ 5

13.   43
    × 6

14.   858
    + 325

15. 6)792

16.   280
    × 8

17.   378
    − 159

18. 8)160

19.   686
   + 528

20.   346
   × 5

21.   572
   − 326

22.   595
   − 271

23.   8,000
   ×   8

24.   464
   × 4

25. Thomas has 52 cents. The candy he wants is 75 cents. How much more money does Thomas need to buy the candy? _____

26. In the parking lot, there are 3 rows of cars, with 15 cars in each row. How many cars are there in the parking lot? _____

27. Silvana has 8 roses and 17 carnations. How many flowers does she have in all? _____

Answers to Practice Set 3A

While these problems may be appropriate for third grade students, feel free to assign some or all of them to any student who needs practice at this level.

This Practice Set emphasizes addition, subtraction, multiplication, and division of whole numbers as well as addition and subtraction of decimals. Note the use of two different multiplication symbols (× and *).

Name   Date   Time

Practice Set 3A

Use your favorite strategies to solve the following problems:

1. $112 + 65$ 177   **2.** $15 * 8$ 120   **3.** $288 \div 9$ 32

4. $458 - 333$ 125   **5.** $276 + 451$ 727   **6.** $934 + 685$ 1,619

7. $197 - 51$ 146   **8.** 22×6 132   **9.** $27 * 3$ 81

10. $2\overline{)188}$ (94)   **11.** $240 \div 4$ 60   **12.** $32{,}116 + 242$ 32,358

13.   15.2   **14.**   70.8   **15.**   27.9
      + 38.7   + 34.5   + 52.2
      53.9   105.3   80.1

16.   79.6   **17.**   7.21   **18.**   42.6
      − 23.5   − 4.03   − 20.3
      56.1   3.18   22.3

19.   747   **20.**   343   **21.**   89.3
      × 6   * 4   − 21.4
      4,482   1,372   67.9

22.   691   **23.** $5\overline{)555}$ 111   **24.** $3\overline{)633}$ 211
      × 2
      1,382

25. Tara had 25 dollars and 25 cents. Her school supplies cost 16 dollars and 23 cents. How much change did she get back? _____ $9.02

26. Sally has 63 stuffed animals in her collection. Sam has three times the stuffed animals that Sally has. How many stuffed animals does Sam have? _____ 189 stuffed animals

27. Jan gave 528 sports cards to her 4 friends. How many cards did each friend get if they shared the cards equally? _____ 132 cards

Write your answers on a separate sheet of paper.   **Practice Sets 95**

Practice Set 3A

Use your favorite strategies to solve the following problems:

1. $112 + 65$

2. $15 * 8$

3. $288 \div 9$

4. $458 - 333$

5. $276 + 451$

6. $934 + 685$

7. $197 - 51$

8. 22×6

9. $27 * 3$

10. $2\overline{)188}$

11. $240 \div 4$

12. $32,116 + 242$

13.
$$\begin{array}{r} 15.2 \\ + 38.7 \\ \hline \end{array}$$

14.
$$\begin{array}{r} 70.8 \\ + 34.5 \\ \hline \end{array}$$

15.
$$\begin{array}{r} 27.9 \\ + 52.2 \\ \hline \end{array}$$

16.
$$\begin{array}{r} 79.6 \\ - 23.5 \\ \hline \end{array}$$

17.
$$\begin{array}{r} 7.21 \\ - 4.03 \\ \hline \end{array}$$

18.
$$\begin{array}{r} 42.6 \\ - 20.3 \\ \hline \end{array}$$

19.
$$\begin{array}{r} 747 \\ \times \ \ 6 \\ \hline \end{array}$$

20.
$$\begin{array}{r} 343 \\ * \ \ 4 \\ \hline \end{array}$$

21.
$$\begin{array}{r} 89.3 \\ - 21.4 \\ \hline \end{array}$$

22.
$$\begin{array}{r} 691 \\ \times \ \ 2 \\ \hline \end{array}$$

23. $5\overline{)555}$

24. $3\overline{)633}$

25. Tara had 25 dollars and 25 cents.
Her school supplies cost 16 dollars and
23 cents. How much change did she get back? _____

26. Sally has 63 stuffed animals in her collection. Sam
has three times the stuffed animals that Sally has.
How many stuffed animals does Sam have? _____

27. Jan gave 528 sports cards to
her 4 friends. How many cards did each
friend get if they shared the cards equally? _____

Write your answers on a separate sheet of paper.

Answers to Practice Set 3B

While these problems may be appropriate for third grade students, feel free to assign some or all of them to any student who needs practice at this level.

This Practice Set emphasizes addition subtraction, multiplication, and division of whole numbers as well as addition and subtraction of decimals. Note the use of two different multiplication symbols (× and ∗) and two different division symbols (÷ and $\overline{)}$).

Name   Date   Time

Practice Set 3B

Use your favorite strategies to solve the following problems:

1. 115 + 56   171   **2.** 17 × 4   68   **3.** 252 ÷ 6   42

4. 547 − 445   102   **5.** 327 − 168   159   **6.** 843 + 823   1,666

7. 179 − 42   137   **8.** 33 × 4   132   **9.** 47 × 6   282

10. $3\overline{)225}$ 75   **11.** 560 ÷ 8   70   **12.** 14,678 + 345   15,023

13.
$$\begin{array}{r} 16.3 \\ + \ 36.1 \\ \hline 52.4 \end{array}$$
14.
$$\begin{array}{r} 80.7 \\ + \ 43.6 \\ \hline 124.3 \end{array}$$
15.
$$\begin{array}{r} 38.9 \\ + \ 24.4 \\ \hline 63.3 \end{array}$$

16.
$$\begin{array}{r} 68.7 \\ - \ 32.5 \\ \hline 36.2 \end{array}$$
17.
$$\begin{array}{r} 8.23 \\ - \ 5.04 \\ \hline 3.19 \end{array}$$
18.
$$\begin{array}{r} 56.8 \\ - \ 20.5 \\ \hline 36.3 \end{array}$$

19.
$$\begin{array}{r} 656 \\ \times \ 4 \\ \hline 2,624 \end{array}$$
20.
$$\begin{array}{r} 232 \\ \times \ 3 \\ \hline 696 \end{array}$$
21.
$$\begin{array}{r} 98.4 \\ - \ 12.5 \\ \hline 85.9 \end{array}$$

22.
$$\begin{array}{r} 781 \\ \times \ 3 \\ \hline 2,343 \end{array}$$
23.
$$\begin{array}{r} 434 \\ \ast \ 8 \\ \hline 3,472 \end{array}$$
24. $7\overline{)147}$ 21

25. Amy had 15 dollars and 75 cents. She spent 6 dollars and 50 cents on her movie ticket. How much money did she have left? $9.25

26. Gina collected 15 pledges for the walk-a-thon. Brian collected six times the pledges that Gina did. How many pledges does Brian have?   90 pledges

27. Ken delivered 884 cases of bottled water to 26 stores. How many cases of water did each store get if they each got the same amount?   34 cases of water

Write your answers on a separate sheet of paper.   **Practice Sets   97**

Practice Set 3B

Use your favorite strategies to solve the following problems:

1. $115 + 56$ **2.** 17×4 **3.** $252 \div 6$

4. $547 - 445$ **5.** $327 - 168$ **6.** $843 + 823$

7. $179 - 42$ **8.** 33×4 **9.** 47×6

10. $3\overline{)225}$ **11.** $560 \div 8$ **12.** $14,678 + 345$

13.
$$\begin{array}{r} 16.3 \\ + \ 36.1 \\ \hline \end{array}$$
14.
$$\begin{array}{r} 80.7 \\ + \ 43.6 \\ \hline \end{array}$$
15.
$$\begin{array}{r} 38.9 \\ + \ 24.4 \\ \hline \end{array}$$

16.
$$\begin{array}{r} 68.7 \\ - \ 32.5 \\ \hline \end{array}$$
17.
$$\begin{array}{r} 8.23 \\ - \ 5.04 \\ \hline \end{array}$$
18.
$$\begin{array}{r} 56.8 \\ - \ 20.5 \\ \hline \end{array}$$

19.
$$\begin{array}{r} 656 \\ \times \ \ 4 \\ \hline \end{array}$$
20.
$$\begin{array}{r} 232 \\ \times \ \ 3 \\ \hline \end{array}$$
21.
$$\begin{array}{r} 98.4 \\ - \ 12.5 \\ \hline \end{array}$$

22.
$$\begin{array}{r} 781 \\ \times \ \ 3 \\ \hline \end{array}$$
23.
$$\begin{array}{r} 434 \\ * \ \ 8 \\ \hline \end{array}$$
24. $7\overline{)147}$

25. Amy had 15 dollars and 75 cents. She spent 6 dollars and 50 cents on her movie ticket. How much money did she have left? _____

26. Gina collected 15 pledges for the walk-a-thon. Brian collected six times the pledges that Gina did. How many pledges does Brian have? _____

27. Ken delivered 884 cases of bottled water to 26 stores. How many cases of water did each store get if they each got the same amount? _____

Answers to Practice Set 4A

While these problems may be appropriate for third grade students, feel free to assign some or all of them to any student who needs practice at this level.

This Practice Set emphasizes addition, subtraction, multiplication, and division of whole numbers and decimals.

Name   Date   Time

Practice Set 4A

Use your favorite strategies to solve the following problems:

1. 205 + 18 223   **2.** 638 – 429 209   **3.** 76.4 – 46.1 30.3

4. 36 × 7 252   **5.** 18,936 + 945 19,881   **6.** 18.1 + 19.9 38

7. 192 ÷ 6 32   **8.** 208 – 49 159   **9.** 3.2 × 2 6.4

10. 336 × 2 672   **11.** 8.36 + 5.01 13.37   **12.** 738 / 9 82

13. 3)141 _47_

14.   59.6
          – 58.7
           0.9

15.   938
          + 945
          1,883

16.   4.1
          ×   3
          12.3

17. 9)783 87

18.   805
          – 249
           556

19. 2)2.8 1.4

20.   96.2
          + 48.9
          145.1

21.   6.03
          – 4.28
           1.75

22. 3)3.6 _1.2_

23.   434
          *   8
          3,472

24.   8.3
          ×   2
          16.6

25. Sam has 252 baseball cards. He wants to share them equally among 3 friends. How many baseball cards does each friend get? _____84 cards_____

26. Julie wants to put 6 ounces of water in each glass. How many glasses can she fill with 42 ounces of water? _____7 glasses_____

27. Ashley has $45.00. Does she have enough to buy a skirt that costs $24.50 and a blouse that costs $17.00? _____yes_____

Write your answers on a separate sheet of paper.   **Practice Sets 99**

Practice Set 4A

Use your favorite strategies to solve the following problems:

1. $205 + 18$

2. $638 - 429$

3. $76.4 - 46.1$

4. 36×7

5. $18{,}936 + 945$

6. $18.1 + 19.9$

7. $192 \div 6$

8. $208 - 49$

9. 3.2×2

10. 336×2

11. $8.36 + 5.01$

12. $738 / 9$

13. $3\overline{)141}$

14.
$$\begin{array}{r} 59.6 \\ -\ 58.7 \end{array}$$

15.
$$\begin{array}{r} 938 \\ +\ 945 \end{array}$$

16.
$$\begin{array}{r} 4.1 \\ \times\ 3 \end{array}$$

17. $9\overline{)783}$

18.
$$\begin{array}{r} 805 \\ -\ 249 \end{array}$$

19. $2\overline{)2.8}$

20.
$$\begin{array}{r} 96.2 \\ +\ 48.9 \end{array}$$

21.
$$\begin{array}{r} 6.03 \\ -\ 4.28 \end{array}$$

22. $3\overline{)3.6}$

23.
$$\begin{array}{r} 434 \\ *\ 8 \end{array}$$

24.
$$\begin{array}{r} 8.3 \\ \times\ 2 \end{array}$$

25. Sam has 252 baseball cards. He wants to share them equally among 3 friends. How many baseball cards does each friend get? _____

26. Julie wants to put 6 ounces of water in each glass. How many glasses can she fill with 42 ounces of water? _____

27. Ashley has $45.00. Does she have enough to buy a skirt that costs $24.50 and a blouse that costs $17.00? _____

Answers to Practice Set 4B

While these problems may be appropriate for third grade students, feel free to assign some or all of them to any student who needs practice at this level.

This Practice Set emphasizes addition, subtraction, multiplication, and division of whole numbers and decimals.

Name   Date   Time

Practice Set 4B

Use your favorite strategies to solve the following problems:

1. 336 + 68 404   **2.** 882 − 796 86   **3.** 8.06 − 6.03 2.03

4. 48 * 7 336   **5.** 19,245 + 998 20,243   **6.** 21.6 + 32.5 54.1

7. 256 ÷ 8 32   **8.** 306 − 59 247   **9.** 4.2 × 2 8.4

10. 448 * 3 1,344   **11.** 9.62 + 4.08 13.7   **12.** 744 / 8 93

13. 4)264 $\overset{66}{}$ **14.**   49.8   **15.**   996
                                           − 48.9   + 958
                                            0.9   1,954

16.   3.1   **17.** 9)837 93   **18.**   932
        × 5   − 248
        15.5   684

19. 2)4.2 2.1   **20.**   87.6   **21.**   8.05
                             + 58.9   − 6.28
                              146.5   1.77

22. 3)3.9 $\overset{1.3}{}$ **23.** 526   **24.**   9.2
                                          * 7   × 3
                                         3,682   27.6

25. Justin wants to give away 87 of his hockey cards to his three brothers. How many cards will each brother get if they share the cards equally? _____29 cards_____

26. Dina has $25.00. Does she have enough to buy a radio that costs $14.79 and a CD that costs $11.25? _____no_____

27. Joshua wants to cut a 56-inch piece of string into pieces that are each 8 inches long. How many 8-inch pieces can he cut? _____7 pieces_____

Write your answers on a separate sheet of paper.   **Practice Sets   101**

Practice Set 4B

Use your favorite strategies to solve the following problems:

1. 336 + 68

2. 882 − 796

3. 8.06 − 6.03

4. 48 * 7

5. 19,245 + 998

6. 21.6 + 32.5

7. 256 ÷ 8

8. 306 − 59

9. 4.2 × 2

10. 448 * 3

11. 9.62 + 4.08

12. 744 / 8

13. 4)264

14.   49.8
     − 48.9

15.   996
    + 958

16.   3.1
    × 5

17. 9)837

18.   932
    − 248

19. 2)4.2

20.   87.6
   + 58.9

21.   8.05
   − 6.28

22. 3)3.9

23.   526
   * 7

24.   9.2
   × 3

25. Justin wants to give away 87 of his hockey cards to his three brothers. How many cards will each brother get if they share the cards equally? _____

26. Dina has $25.00. Does she have enough to buy a radio that costs $14.79 and a CD that costs $11.25? _____

27. Joshua wants to cut a 56-inch piece of string into pieces that are each 8 inches long. How many 8-inch pieces can he cut? _____

Answers to Practice Set 5A

While these problems may be appropriate for third grade students, feel free to assign some or all of them to any student who needs practice at this level.

This Practice Set emphasizes addition, subtraction, multiplication, and division of whole numbers as well as addition and subtraction of decimals and fractions.

Name _____ Date _____ Time _____

Practice Set 5A

Use your favorite strategies to solve the following problems:

1. 336 + 291 627

2. 786 − 29 757

3. 7.2 × 8 57.6

4. 6,231 − 746
5,485

5. 4.32 − 3.05 1.27

6. $\frac{2}{4} + \frac{1}{4}$ $\frac{3}{4}$

7. 428 * 7 2,996

8. 16,328 + 822
17,150

9. 600 ÷ 8 75

10. 60 × 20 1,200

11. $\frac{4}{8} + \frac{3}{8}$ $\frac{7}{8}$

12. $\frac{2}{3} − \frac{1}{3}$ $\frac{1}{3}$

13. 8.06
− 6.08
1.98

14. 306
* 7
2,142

15. 49.1
+ 52.9
102

16. 20)‾40 2

17. $\frac{4}{5} − \frac{2}{5}$ $\frac{2}{5}$

18. 30
× 60
1,800

19. 2.1
4)‾8.4

20. $\frac{3}{9} − \frac{2}{9}$ $\frac{1}{9}$

21. $\frac{6}{8} + \frac{1}{8}$ $\frac{7}{8}$

22. 3,321
− 456
2,865

23. 3.1
3)‾9.3

24. 321.6
+ 456.2
777.8

25. David has a book that holds 9 baseball cards on each page. How many cards can he put in the book if the book has 10 pages? ____90 cards____

26. The pet store has 10 birds for sale. Half of the birds are canaries. How many of the birds are canaries? ____5 birds____

27. Samuel caught a fish that was 26 inches long. Carol caught a fish that was 42 inches long. How much longer was Carol's fish? __16 inches longer__

Write your answers on a separate sheet of paper.

Practice Set 5A

Use your favorite strategies to solve the following problems:

1. 336 + 291

2. 786 − 29

3. 7.2 × 8

4. 6,231 − 746

5. 4.32 − 3.05

6. $\frac{2}{4} + \frac{1}{4}$

7. 428 * 7

8. 16,328 + 822

9. 600 ÷ 8

10. 60 × 20

11. $\frac{4}{8} + \frac{3}{8}$

12. $\frac{2}{3} - \frac{1}{3}$

13.
$$\begin{array}{r} 8.06 \\ -\ 6.08 \\ \hline \end{array}$$

14.
$$\begin{array}{r} 306 \\ *\ \ 7 \\ \hline \end{array}$$

15.
$$\begin{array}{r} 49.1 \\ +\ 52.9 \\ \hline \end{array}$$

16. $20\overline{)40}$

17. $\frac{4}{5} - \frac{2}{5}$

18.
$$\begin{array}{r} 30 \\ \times\ 60 \\ \hline \end{array}$$

19. $4\overline{)8.4}$

20. $\frac{3}{9} - \frac{2}{9}$

21. $\frac{6}{8} + \frac{1}{8}$

22.
$$\begin{array}{r} 3,321 \\ -\ 456 \\ \hline \end{array}$$

23. $3\overline{)9.3}$

24.
$$\begin{array}{r} 321.6 \\ +\ 456.2 \\ \hline \end{array}$$

25. David has a book that holds 9 baseball cards on each page. How many cards can he put in the book if the book has 10 pages? _____

26. The pet store has 10 birds for sale. Half of the birds are canaries. How many of the birds are canaries? _____

27. Samuel caught a fish that was 26 inches long. Carol caught a fish that was 42 inches long. How much longer was Carol's fish? _____

Answers to Practice Set 5B

While these problems may be appropriate for third grade students, feel free to assign some or all of them to any student who needs practice at this level.

This Practice Set emphasizes addition, subtraction, multiplication, and division of whole numbers as well as addition and subtraction of decimals and fractions.

Name   Date   Time

Practice Set 5B

Use your favorite strategies to solve the following problems:

1. $428 + 329$ 757 **2.** $832 - 85$ 747 **3.** 7.9×7 55.3

4. $5{,}321 - 846$ **5.** $3.46 - 2.09$ 1.37 **6.** $\frac{1}{3} + \frac{1}{3}$ $\frac{2}{3}$
      $4{,}475$

7. $521 * 8$ $4{,}168$ **8.** $15{,}299 + 764$ **9.** $532 \div 7$ 76
                            $16{,}063$

10. 70×30 $2{,}100$ **11.** $\frac{1}{6} + \frac{4}{6}$ $\frac{5}{6}$ **12.** $\frac{3}{4} - \frac{2}{4}$ $\frac{1}{4}$

13. $\begin{array}{r} 9.03 \\ -\ 6.05 \\ \hline 2.98 \end{array}$ **14.** $\begin{array}{r} 4.8 \\ *\ 8 \\ \hline 38.4 \end{array}$ **15.** $\begin{array}{r} 36.8 \\ +\ 67.3 \\ \hline 104.1 \end{array}$

16. $30\overline{)60}$ 2 **17.** $\begin{array}{r} \frac{4}{6} \\ -\ \frac{3}{6} \\ \hline \end{array}$ $\frac{1}{6}$ **18.** $\begin{array}{r} 40 \\ \times\ 80 \\ \hline 3{,}200 \end{array}$

19. $3\overline{)9.6}$ 3.2 **20.** $\begin{array}{r} \frac{4}{7} \\ -\ \frac{2}{7} \\ \hline \end{array}$ $\frac{2}{7}$ **21.** $\begin{array}{r} \frac{6}{9} \\ +\ \frac{2}{9} \\ \hline \end{array}$ $\frac{8}{9}$

22. $\begin{array}{r} 4{,}326 \\ -\ 652 \\ \hline 3{,}674 \end{array}$ **23.** $2\overline{)4.6}$ 2.3 **24.** $\begin{array}{r} 423.8 \\ +\ 372.1 \\ \hline 795.9 \end{array}$

25. Gail has 412 hockey cards and 843 basketball cards. How many more basketball cards than hockey cards does she have?   __431 cards__

26. The third grade class went to the park. They counted 12 kites flying. Half of them were blue. How many kites were blue?   __6__

27. Sheilia bought 4 boxes of markers. Each box has 8 markers. How many markers did Sheila buy?   __32 markers__

Write your answers on a separate sheet of paper.   **Practice Sets   105**

Practice Set 5B

Use your favorite strategies to solve the following problems:

1. 428 + 329

2. 832 − 85

3. 7.9 × 7

4. 5,321 − 846

5. 3.46 − 2.09

6. $\frac{1}{3} + \frac{1}{3}$

7. 521 * 8

8. 15,299 + 764

9. 532 ÷ 7

10. 70 × 30

11. $\frac{1}{6} + \frac{4}{6}$

12. $\frac{3}{4} - \frac{2}{4}$

13.   9.03
      − 6.05

14.   4.8
      * 8

15.   36.8
      + 67.3

16. 30)‾60

17. $\frac{4}{6}$
      $- \frac{3}{6}$

18.   40
      × 80

19. 3)‾9.6

20. $\frac{4}{7}$
      $- \frac{2}{7}$

21. $\frac{6}{9}$
      $+ \frac{2}{9}$

22.   4,326
      − 652

23. 2)‾4.6

24.   423.8
      + 372.1

25. Gail has 412 hockey cards and 843 basketball cards. How many more basketball cards than hockey cards does she have? _____

26. The third grade class went to the park. They counted 12 kites flying. Half of them were blue. How many kites were blue? _____

27. Sheilia bought 4 boxes of markers. Each box has 8 markers. How many markers did Sheila buy? _____

Answers to Practice Set 6A

While these problems may be appropriate for fourth grade students, feel free to assign some or all of them to any student who needs practice at this level.

This Practice Set emphasizes addition, subtraction, multiplication, and division of whole numbers. Note the use of two different multiplication symbols ($\times$ and $*$) and two different division symbols ($\div$ and $\overline{)}$).

Name   Date   Time

Practice Set 6A

Use your favorite strategies to solve the following problems:

1. 53 * 8 424   **2.** 648 − 537 111   **3.** 276 ÷ 4 69

4. 49 * 7 343   **5.** 684 ÷ 9 76   **6.** 6 * 54 324

7. 125 + 467 592   **8.** 28 * 6 168   **9.** 3,075 − 410 2,665

10. 1,500 ÷ 15 100   **11.** 4,600 ÷ 20 230   **12.** 73 * 19 1,387

13. 3)1,683 561

14. 4,514
     + 838
     5,352

15. 3,914
     − 467
     3,447

16. 612
    × 7
   4,284

17. 2,091
    − 1,368
     723

18. 9,000 ÷ 30 300

19. 313
    × 8
   2,504

20. 46
   × 70
  3,220

21. 5)1,175 235

22. 58
   × 21
  1,218

23. 5,001
    − 2,999
    2,002

24. 10,921
     − 7,556
     3,365

25. At the bake sale, the third grade collected $125, and the fourth grade collected $210. How much money did the two grades earn in all? _____ $335 _____

26. At the recycling center there were 8,310 cans. If 4,822 cans were crushed, how many cans are uncrushed? _____ 3,488 cans _____

27. The parade has 525 marchers. If they march 5 to a line, how many lines of marchers will there be? _____ 105 lines _____

Write your answers on a separate sheet of paper.   **Practice Sets 107**

Practice Set 6A

Use your favorite strategies to solve the following problems:

1. 53 * 8

2. 648 − 537

3. 276 ÷ 4

4. 49 * 7

5. 684 ÷ 9

6. 6 * 54

7. 125 + 467

8. 28 * 6

9. 3,075 − 410

10. 1,500 ÷ 15

11. 4,600 ÷ 20

12. 73 * 19

13. 3)$\overline{1,683}$

14. 4,514
+ 838

15. 3,914
− 467

16. 612
× 7

17. 2,091
− 1,368

18. 9,000 ÷ 30

19. 313
× 8

20. 46
× 70

21. 5)$\overline{1,175}$

22. 58
× 21

23. 5,001
− 2,999

24. 10,921
− 7,556

25. At the bake sale, the third grade collected $125, and the fourth grade collected $210. How much money did the two grades earn in all? _____

26. At the recycling center there were 8,310 cans. If 4,822 cans were crushed, how many cans are uncrushed? _____

27. The parade has 525 marchers. If they march 5 to a line, how many lines of marchers will there be? _____

Answers to Practice Set 6B

While these problems may be appropriate for fourth grade students, feel free to assign some or all of them to any student who needs practice at this level.

This Practice Set emphasizes addition, subtraction, multiplication, and division of whole numbers. Note the use of two different multiplication symbols (× and *) and two different division symbols (÷ and ⟌).

Name   Date   Time

Practice Set 6B

Use your favorite strategies to solve the following problems:

1. 35 * 7 245   **2.** 468 – 377 91   **3.** 726 ÷ 2 363

4. 92 * 5 460   **5.** 639 ÷ 9 71   **6.** 4 * 85 340

7. 253 + 431 684   **8.** 8 * 36 288   **9.** 8,739 – 123 8,616

10. 2,400 ÷ 12 200   **11.** 5,400 ÷ 60 90   **12.** 47 * 96 4,512

13. $\overset{456}{4\overline{)1,824}}$

14. 4,692
    + 1,921
    6,613

15. 3,512
    – 219
    3,293

16. 265
    × 8
    2,120

17. 6,407
    – 2,315
    4,092

18. 8,000 ÷ 20 400

19. 599
    × 2
    1,198

20. 64
    × 50
    3,200

21. $\overset{192}{6\overline{)1,152}}$

22. 29
    * 43
    1,247

23. 3,001
    – 1,853
    1,148

24. 12,021
    – 1,436
    10,585

25. Sally sold $325 worth of candy bars in the school fundraiser. Marla sold $177. How much money did the two girls collect for the school? _____ $502 _____

26. Regina filled the giant gumball machine with 3,500 gumballs. If 1,225 gumballs were bought, how many are left?
    2,275 gumballs

27. Eight people will fit at each round table in the banquet hall. If there are 184 people, how many tables need to be set?
    23 tables

Write your answers on a separate sheet of paper.   **Practice Sets   109**

Practice Set 6B

Use your favorite strategies to solve the following problems:

1. 35 * 7

2. 468 − 377

3. 726 ÷ 2

4. 92 * 5

5. 639 ÷ 9

6. 4 * 85

7. 253 + 431

8. 8 * 36

9. 8,739 − 123

10. 2,400 ÷ 12

11. 5,400 ÷ 60

12. 47 * 96

13. 4)1,824

14. 4,692
    +1,921

15. 3,512
    − 219

16. 265
   × 8

17. 6,407
   − 2,315

18. 8,000 ÷ 20

19. 599
   × 2

20. 64
   × 50

21. 6)1,152

22. 29
   * 43

23. 3,001
   − 1,853

24. 12,021
   − 1,436

25. Sally sold $325 worth of candy bars in the school fundraiser. Marla sold $177. How much money did the two girls collect for the school? _____

26. Regina filled the giant gumball machine with 3,500 gumballs. If 1,225 gumballs were bought, how many are left?

_____

27. Eight people will fit at each round table in the banquet hall. If there are 184 people, how many tables need to be set?

_____

Answers to Practice Set 7A

While these problems may be appropriate for fourth grade students, feel free to assign some or all of them to any student who needs practice at this level.

This Practice Set emphasizes addition, subtraction, multiplication, and division of whole numbers and decimals. Note the use of two different multiplication symbols ($\times$ and $*$) and three different division symbols (/ and $\div$ and $\overline{)}$).

Name   Date   Time

Practice Set 7A

Use your favorite strategies to solve the following problems:

1. 618 $*$ 2 1,236   2. 190 + 527 717   3. 648 − 415 233

4. 5,400 / 60 90   5. 4,000 $\div$ 80 50   6. 325 $*$ 4 1,300

7. 82.9 − 6.3 76.6   8. 44.1 + 26.2 70.3   9. 318.5 + 254.9 573.4

10. 1,872 − 531 1,341   11. 180 / 20 9   12. 3,164 $*$ 2 6,328

13. $90\overline{)8{,}100}$ 90

14. $50\overline{)2{,}000}$ 40

15.   6,173
    + 1,094
    7,267

16.   51.47
    + 83.16
    134.63

17.   803
    $\times$ 11
    8,833

18.   46.17
    $\times$ 3
    138.51

19.   9,108
    − 4,613
    4,495

20.   50.07
    − 14.43
    35.64

21. 2,138
    − 499
    1,639

22. 1,407
    $\times$ 15
    21,105

23. 6,029
    $\times$ 10
    60,290

24.   50.00
    − 29.87
    20.13

25. The grocery-store display has 15 rows of 21 cans each. How many cans are in the display? _____ 315 cans _____

26. On Saturday, 1,327 people came to the play. On Sunday, 1,109 people came to the play. How many people in all came to the play on those two days? _____ 2,436 people _____

27. The hiking club earned $1,209 from its walk-a-thon. If the expenses for the walk-a-thon were $138, how much profit did club members make? _____ $1,071 _____

Write your answers on a separate sheet of paper.   **Practice Sets 111**

Practice Set 7A

Use your favorite strategies to solve the following problems:

1. 618 * 2

2. 190 + 527

3. 648 − 415

4. 5,400 / 60

5. 4,000 ÷ 80

6. 325 * 4

7. 82.9 − 6.3

8. 44.1 + 26.2

9. 318.5 + 254.9

10. 1,872 − 531

11. 180 / 20

12. 3,164 * 2

13. 90)8,100

14. 50)2,000

15.   6,173
    + 1,094

16.   51.47
    + 83.16

17.   803
    × 11

18. 46.17
    ×   3

19.   9,108
    − 4,613

20.   50.07
    − 14.43

21. 2,138
    − 499

22. 1,407
    × 15

23. 6,029
    × 10

24.   50.00
    − 29.87

25. The grocery-store display has 15 rows of 21 cans each. How many cans are in the display? _____

26. On Saturday, 1,327 people came to the play. On Sunday, 1,109 people came to the play. How many people in all came to the play on those two days? _____

27. The hiking club earned $1,209 from its walk-a-thon. If the expenses for the walk-a-thon were $138, how much profit did club members make? _____

Answers to Practice Set 7B

While these problems may be appropriate for fourth grade students, feel free to assign some or all of them to any student who needs practice at this level.

This Practice Set emphasizes addition, subtraction, multiplication, and division of whole numbers and decimals. Note the use of two different multiplication symbols ($\times$ and $*$) and three different division symbols (/ and $\div$ and $\overline{)}$).

Name _____ Date _____ Time _____

Practice Set 7B

Use your favorite strategies to solve the following problems:

1. $861 * 3$ 2,583　　**2.** $280 + 634$ 914　　**3.** $788 - 542$ 246

4. $3,500 / 50$ 70　　**5.** $80,000 \div 20$ 4,000　　**6.** $48.2 * 6$ 289.2

7. $92.3 - 8.7$ 83.6　　**8.** $75.4 + 68.8$ 144.2　　**9.** $231.5 + 454.5$ 686

10. $2,613 - 462$ 2151　　**11.** $270 / 30$ 9　　**12.** $5,642 * 3$ 16,926

13. $70\overline{)4,900}$ 70　　**14.** $40\overline{)5,200}$ 130

15.
$$\begin{array}{r} 4,586 \\ + 1,320 \\ \hline 5,906 \end{array}$$

16.
$$\begin{array}{r} 47.51 \\ + 16.83 \\ \hline 64.34 \end{array}$$

17.
$$\begin{array}{r} 704 \\ \times \ 13 \\ \hline 9,152 \end{array}$$

18.
$$\begin{array}{r} 65.12 \\ \times \quad 4 \\ \hline 260.48 \end{array}$$

19.
$$\begin{array}{r} 8,510 \\ - 6,349 \\ \hline 2,161 \end{array}$$

20.
$$\begin{array}{r} 40.06 \\ - 18.62 \\ \hline 21.44 \end{array}$$

21.
$$\begin{array}{r} 5,431 \\ - \quad 633 \\ \hline 4,798 \end{array}$$

22.
$$\begin{array}{r} 1,357 \\ \times \quad 18 \\ \hline 24,426 \end{array}$$

23.
$$\begin{array}{r} 2,960 \\ \times \quad 11 \\ \hline 32,560 \end{array}$$

24.
$$\begin{array}{r} 80.00 \\ - 58.85 \\ \hline 21.15 \end{array}$$

25. The children's library section has 32 shelves with 25 books on each shelf. How many books are in the children's section? ___800 books___

26. An office clerk made 1,237 photocopies on Monday. On Tuesday, the same clerk made 989 copies. How many copies did the clerk make in all? ___2,226 copies___

27. In January, Alice spent $376.23 on her family groceries. In February, she spent $401.67. How much was her grocery bill for January and February altogether? ___$777.90___

Write your answers on a separate sheet of paper.　　**Practice Sets 113**

Practice Set 7B

Use your favorite strategies to solve the following problems:

1. 861 * 3

2. 280 + 634

3. 788 − 542

4. 3,500 / 50

5. 80,000 ÷ 20

6. 48.2 * 6

7. 92.3 − 8.7

8. 75.4 + 68.8

9. 231.5 + 454.5

10. 2,613 − 462

11. 270 / 30

12. 5,642 * 3

13. 70)‾4,900

14. 40)‾5,200

15.   4,586
    + 1,320

16.   47.51
    + 16.83

17.   704
    × 13

18.   65.12
   ×   4

19.   8,510
    − 6,349

20.   40.06
    − 18.62

21.   5,431
    −   633

22.   1,357
   ×   18

23.   2,960
   ×   11

24.   80.00
    − 58.85

25. The children's library section has 32 shelves with 25 books on each shelf. How many books are in the children's section? _____

26. An office clerk made 1,237 photocopies on Monday. On Tuesday, the same clerk made 989 copies. How many copies did the clerk make in all? _____

27. In January, Alice spent $376.23 on her family groceries. In February, she spent $401.67. How much was her grocery bill for January and February altogether?

_____

Answers to Practice Set 8A

While these problems may be appropriate for fourth grade students, feel free to assign some or all of them to any student who needs practice at this level.

This Practice Set emphasizes addition, subtraction, multiplication, and division of whole numbers and decimals. Note the use of two different multiplication symbols (× and *) and three different division symbols (/ and ÷ and $\overline{)}$).

Practice Set 8A

Use your favorite strategies to solve the following problems:

1. 17.4 + 58.9 76.3   **2.** 91.9 − 58.2 33.7   **3.** 18.2 * 40 728

4. 415.20 − 311.11   **5.** 4.16 ÷ 8 0.52   **6.** 56.23 − 51.28 4.95
          104.09

7. 9,275 / 25 371   **8.** 215 * 30 6,450   **9.** 390 ÷ 13 30

10. 289.6 + 528.1 817.7 **11.** 336 * 20 6,720   **12.** 5.6 / 8 0.7

13.   639.23   **14.**   6,453   **15.** 24)$\overline{4,824}$ 201
     − 462.22   + 4,561
      177.01   11,014

16.   9.097   **17.**   258.36   **18.**   9,654.78
     − 8.456   + 369.96   − 564.32
     0.641   628.32   9,090.46

19.   8.2   **20.**   2,356   **21.**   250
     × 2.5   − 1,245   × 7
     20.5   1,111   1,750

22. 15)$\overline{6,030}$ 402   **23.**   698.33   **24.** 4)$\overline{57.6}$ 14.4
                       − 321.23
                       377.10

25. 250 couples came to the benefit dinner. Tickets cost $22 per person. How much money did the benefit raise? _____$11,000.00_____

26. At the dinner, people were seated at tables of 10. How many tables were there? _____50 tables_____

27. The food for the benefit cost $10.00 per person. How much money did the dinner raise, after expenses? _____$6,000.00_____

Practice Set 8A

Use your favorite strategies to solve the following problems:

1. 17.4 + 58.9   **2.** 91.9 − 58.2   **3.** 18.2 ∗ 40

4. 415.20 − 311.11 **5.** 4.16 ÷ 8   **6.** 56.23 − 51.28

7. 9,275 / 25   **8.** 215 ∗ 30   **9.** 390 ÷ 13

10. 289.6 + 528.1   **11.** 336 ∗ 20   **12.** 5.6 / 8

13. 639.23   **14.** 6,453   **15.** 24)4,824
   − 462.22   + 4,561

16. 9.097   **17.** 258.36   **18.** 9,654.78
   − 8.456   + 369.96   − 564.32

19. 8.2   **20.** 2,356   **21.** 250
  × 2.5   − 1,245   × 7

22. 15)6,030   **23.** 698.33   **24.** 4)57.6
           − 321.23

25. 250 couples came to the benefit
dinner. Tickets cost $22 per person.
How much money did the benefit raise? _____

26. At the dinner, people were seated at
tables of 10. How many tables were there? _____

27. The food for the benefit cost $10.00
per person. How much money
did the dinner raise, after expenses? _____

Answers to Practice Set 8B

While these problems may be appropriate for fourth grade students, feel free to assign some or all of them to any student who needs practice at this level.

This Practice Set emphasizes addition, subtraction, multiplication, and division of whole numbers and decimals. Note the use of two different multiplication symbols (× and *) and three different division symbols (/ and ÷ and $\overline{)}$).

Name   Date   Time

Practice Set 8B

Use your favorite strategies to solve the following problems:

1. 14.6 + 89.5 104.1   **2.** 81.7 – 63.1 18.6   **3.** 15.4 * 60 924

4. 541.02 – 131.22   **5.** 36.4 ÷ 7 5.2   **6.** 65.32 – 21.85 43.47
         409.8

7. 8,225 / 35 235   **8.** 517 * 50 25,850   **9.** 588 ÷ 14 42

10. 398.4 + 675.2   **11.** 532 * 40 21,280   **12.** 7.2 / 9 0.8
       1,073.6

13.   458.25   **14.**   6,407   **15.** $\overset{72}{47\overline{)3,384}}$
    – 264.18   + 2,317
    194.07   8,724

16.   83.129   **17.**   740.05   **18.**   8,423.85
    – 7.604   + 143.15   – 654.23
    75.525   883.2   7,769.62

19.   5.4   **20.**   4,780   **21.**   540
    × 8.6   – 2,196   × 8
    46.44   2,584   4,320

22. $19\overline{)3,591}$ 189   **23.**   1,512.63   **24.** $7\overline{)52.5}$ 7.5
                 – 329.18
                 1,183.45

25. 120 people attended the play each night on Friday and Saturday. Tickets cost $26.75 per person. How much money did the play take in over the two nights? _____ $6,420 _____

26. There were 8 rows of seats in the theater. In order to accommodate 120 people, how many seats were in each row? __ 15 seats per row __

27. $12.00 of each theater ticket was donated to charity at the end of the weekend. How much money did the charity receive? _____ $2,880 _____

Write your answers on a separate sheet of paper.   **Practice Sets**   117

Practice Set 8B

Use your favorite strategies to solve the following problems:

1. $14.6 + 89.5$ **2.** $81.7 - 63.1$ **3.** $15.4 * 60$

4. $541.02 - 131.22$ **5.** $36.4 \div 7$ **6.** $65.32 - 21.85$

7. $8,225 / 35$ **8.** $517 * 50$ **9.** $588 \div 14$

10. $398.4 + 675.2$ **11.** $532 * 40$ **12.** $7.2 / 9$

13. $\begin{aligned}458.25 \\ -\,264.18\end{aligned}$ **14.** $\begin{aligned}6,407 \\ +\,2,317\end{aligned}$ **15.** $47\overline{)3,384}$

16. $\begin{aligned}83.129 \\ -\ \ 7.604\end{aligned}$ **17.** $\begin{aligned}740.05 \\ +\,143.15\end{aligned}$ **18.** $\begin{aligned}8,423.85 \\ -\ \ 654.23\end{aligned}$

19. $\begin{aligned}5.4 \\ \times\,8.6\end{aligned}$ **20.** $\begin{aligned}4,780 \\ -\,2,196\end{aligned}$ **21.** $\begin{aligned}540 \\ \times\ \ 8\end{aligned}$

22. $19\overline{)3,591}$ **23.** $\begin{aligned}1,512.63 \\ -\ \ 329.18\end{aligned}$ **24.** $7\overline{)52.5}$

25. 120 people attended the play each night on Friday and Saturday. Tickets cost $26.75 per person. How much money did the play take in over the two nights? _____

26. There were 8 rows of seats in the theater. In order to accommodate 120 people, how many seats were in each row? _____

27. $12.00 of each theater ticket was donated to charity at the end of the weekend. How much money did the charity receive? _____

Write your answers on a separate sheet of paper. **Practice Sets 117**

Answers to Practice Set 9A

While these problems may be appropriate for fourth grade students, feel free to assign some or all of them to any student who needs practice at this level.

This Practice Set emphasizes addition, subtraction, multiplication, and division of decimals. Note the use of two different multiplication symbols ($\times$ and $*$) and three different division symbols ($/$ and $\div$ and $\overline{)}$).

Name   Date   Time

Practice Set 9A

Use your favorite strategies to solve the following problems:

1. 82.6 – 78.9 3.7   **2.** 466.8 + 935.4   **3.** 516.7 + 621.5 1,138.2
                                              1,402.2

4. 16.8 $*$ 80 1,344   **5.** 8.054 – 6.989   **6.** 4.24 / 8 0.53
                                              1.065

7. 6.3 $\times$ 8.3 52.29   **8.** 42.86 $\div$ 2 21.43   **9.** 349.68 + 25.62 375.3

                                                                    0.91
10. 546.98 – 336.55   **11.** 12.8 $*$ 41 524.8   **12.** 9$\overline{)8.19}$
            210.43
      1.03
13. 7$\overline{)7.21}$ **14.**   8,365.21   **15.**   6,289.16
                                    – 2,478.64   + 998.96
                                    5,886.57   7,288.12

16.   17.6   **17.**   638.659   **18.**   8,342.96
        $\times$ 14   + 36.231   – 438.87
      246.4   674.89   7,904.09
19. 2$\overline{)8.04}$ 4.02   **20.**   9.8   **21.**   333.21
                                      $*$ 7.6   – 298.99
                                    74.48   34.22

22.   4,526.321   **23.** 9$\overline{)0.945}$ 0.105   **24.**   13.6
        + 86.213 $\times$ 51
      4,612.534   693.6

25. Tom is going shopping. Each of his two children needs a pair of shoelaces and a toothbrush. The shoelaces cost $1.08 for one pair and each toothbrush costs $0.89. How much is Tom going to spend on these items?
   <u> $3.94   </u>

26. If Tom brings $10.00 with him, will he have enough money to buy the items? If so, how much change will he receive?
   <u>   Yes, $6.06   </u>

27. How much would it cost Tom if only one of his children needed the items?
   <u> $1.97   </u>

Write your answers on a separate sheet of paper.   **Practice Sets 119**

Practice Set 9A

Use your favorite strategies to solve the following problems:

1. $82.6 - 78.9$

2. $466.8 + 935.4$

3. $516.7 + 621.5$

4. $16.8 * 80$

5. $8.054 - 6.989$

6. $4.24 / 8$

7. 6.3×8.3

8. $42.86 \div 2$

9. $349.68 + 25.62$

10. $546.98 - 336.55$

11. $12.8 * 41$

12. $9\overline{)8.19}$

13. $7\overline{)7.21}$

14.
$$8,365.21$$
$$- \; 2,478.64$$

15.
$$6,289.16$$
$$+ \;\; 998.96$$

16.
$$17.6$$
$$\times \;\; 14$$

17.
$$638.659$$
$$+ \;\; 36.231$$

18.
$$8,342.96$$
$$- \;\; 438.87$$

19. $2\overline{)8.04}$

20.
$$9.8$$
$$* \; 7.6$$

21.
$$333.21$$
$$- \;\; 298.99$$

22.
$$4,526.321$$
$$+ \;\;\; 86.213$$

23. $9\overline{)0.945}$

24.
$$13.6$$
$$\times \; 51$$

25. Tom is going shopping. Each of his two children needs a pair of shoelaces and a toothbrush. The shoelaces cost $1.08 for one pair and each toothbrush costs $0.89. How much is Tom going to spend on these items?

_____

26. If Tom brings $10.00 with him, will he have enough money to buy the items? If so, how much change will he receive?

_____

27. How much would it cost Tom if only one of his children needed the items?

_____

Answers to Practice Set 9B

While these problems may be appropriate for fourth grade students, feel free to assign some or all of them to any student who needs practice at this level.

This Practice Set emphasizes addition, subtraction, multiplication, and division of decimals. Note the use of two different multiplication symbols (× and *) and three different division symbols (/ and ÷ and $\overline{)}$).

Name   Date   Time

Practice Set 9B

Use your favorite strategies to solve the following problems:

1. 94.8 − 85.9 8.9   **2.** 398.6 + 874.8   **3.** 628.3 + 745.2 1,373.5
                          1,273.4

4. 19.7 * 70 1,379   **5.** 10.27 ÷ 7.9 1.3   **6.** 10.15 / 7   1.45

7. 7.6 × 6.3 47.88   **8.** 96.39 ÷ 3 32.13   **9.** 628.56 + 36.88 665.44

10. 738.76 − 426.62   **11.** 10.6 * 31 328.6   **12.** 5)3.55 0.71

            312.14

13. 9)9.81 1.09   **14.**   9,221.36   **15.**   5,321.28
                                    − 4,882.57   + 899.89
                                     4,338.79   6,221.17

16.   18.2   **17.**   728.411   **18.**   7,968.87
        × 12   + 39.689   − 525.28
        218.4   768.1   7,443.59

19. 3)9.06 3.02   **20.**   8.6   **21.**   421.11
                                     * 6.9   − 398.98
                                     59.34   22.13

22. 6,298.456   **23.** 7)0.728 0.104   **24.**   14.8
      + 78.965   * 61
      6,377.421   902.8

25. How much money, without tax, would I
        need for 4 VCR tapes that cost $3.25 each? _____ $13.00 _____

26. Would I have enough money if I brought
        $15.00 with me to purchase the tapes? If so,
        how much change would I receive? _____ yes, $2.00 _____

27. Ms. Jackson wants to buy 5 boxes of crayons. A box of 64 crayons
        costs $3.99. If Ms. Jackson has $18.00, does she have enough
        to purchase the 5 boxes?
        _____ no _____

Write your answers on a separate sheet of paper.   **Practice Sets   121**

Practice Set 9B

Use your favorite strategies to solve the following problems:

1. 94.8 − 85.9

2. 398.6 + 874.8

3. 628.3 + 745.2

4. 19.7 * 70

5. 10.27 ÷ 7.9

6. 10.15 / 7

7. 7.6 × 6.3

8. 96.39 ÷ 3

9. 628.56 + 36.88

10. 738.76 − 426.62

11. 10.6 * 31

12. 5)3.55

13. 9)9.81

14.   9,221.36
     − 4,882.57

15.   5,321.28
     + 899.89

16.   18.2
    × 12

17.   728.411
    + 39.689

18.   7,968.87
    − 525.28

19. 3)9.06

20.   8.6
   * 6.9

21.   421.11
    − 398.98

22. 6,298.456
  + 78.965

23. 7)0.728

24.   14.8
  * 61

25. How much money, without tax, would I
need for 4 VCR tapes that cost $3.25 each?_____

26. Would I have enough money if I brought
$15.00 with me to purchase the tapes? If so,
how much change would I receive?_____

27. Ms. Jackson wants to buy 5 boxes of crayons. A box of 64 crayons
costs $3.99. If Ms. Jackson has $18.00, does she have enough
to purchase the 5 boxes?

_____

Write your answers on a separate sheet of paper.

Answers to Practice Set 10A

While these problems may be appropriate for fourth grade students, feel free to assign some or all of them to any student who needs practice at this level.

This Practice Set emphasizes addition, subtraction, multiplication, and division of whole numbers, decimals and fractions. Note the use of two different multiplication symbols ($\times$ and $*$) and three different division symbols (/ and $\div$ and $\overline{)}$).

Name   Date   Time

Practice Set 10A

Use your favorite strategies to solve the following problems:

1. $336 * 8$ 2,688   **2.** $628.22 + 54.34$ **3.** $4,322 - 3,989$ 333
682.56

4. $6,300 / 70$ 90   **5.** $13,978 + 1,694$ **6.** 70.4×2.1 147.84
15,672

7. $4,321.65 - 3,898.41$ **8.** $3\overline{)1,623}$ **9.** $8,292 - 4,315$ 3,977
423.24   541

10. $\frac{9}{12} + \frac{2}{12}$ $\frac{11}{12}$ **11.** $21.2 * 5.4$ 114.48   **12.** $25\overline{)2,050}$ 82

13. $7\overline{)2.45}$ 0.35   **14.** $\begin{array}{r} 28,931 \\ +\ 16,258 \\ \hline 45,189 \end{array}$ **15.** $\begin{array}{r} \frac{10}{12} \\ -\ \frac{8}{12} \\ \hline \end{array}$ $\frac{2}{12}$, or $\frac{1}{6}$

16. $28\overline{)448}$ 16   **17.** $\frac{1}{4} \times \frac{1}{2}$ $\frac{1}{8}$ **18.** $\begin{array}{r} \frac{10}{16} \\ -\ \frac{8}{16} \\ \hline \end{array}$ $\frac{2}{16}$, or $\frac{1}{8}$

19. $\frac{1}{3} \div \frac{2}{3}$ $\frac{3}{6}$, or $\frac{1}{2}$ **20.** $\begin{array}{r} 12.054 \\ +\ 96.998 \\ \hline 109.052 \end{array}$ **21.** $\begin{array}{r} 321.43 \\ -\ 286.56 \\ \hline 34.87 \end{array}$

22. $\begin{array}{r} \frac{3}{4} \\ *\ \frac{1}{3} \\ \hline \end{array}$ $\frac{3}{12}$, or $\frac{1}{4}$ **23.** $\begin{array}{r} \frac{24}{30} \\ +\ \frac{3}{30} \\ \hline \end{array}$ $\frac{27}{30}$ **24.** $\begin{array}{r} 9.9 \\ *\ 81 \\ \hline 801.9 \end{array}$

25. 129 people came to the school's spaghetti supper. Tickets cost $7.50 per person. How much money did the spaghetti supper make? _____ $967.50

26. The school paid $224.36 for the food that was served. The people who ran the supper volunteered their time. How much did the supper make, after expenses? _____ $743.14

27. The student aide made 1,267 photocopies on Monday. On Tuesday, the same aide made 1,209 copies. On Wednesday, he made 382 copies. How many copies did he make in all? _____ 2,858 copies

Write your answers on a separate sheet of paper.   **Practice Sets   123**

Practice Set 10A

Use your favorite strategies to solve the following problems:

1. $336 * 8$ **2.** $628.22 + 54.34$ **3.** $4,322 - 3,989$

4. $6,300 / 70$ **5.** $13,978 + 1,694$ **6.** 70.4×2.1

7. $4,321.65 - 3,898.41$ **8.** $3\overline{)1,623}$ **9.** $8,292 - 4,315$

10. $\frac{9}{12} + \frac{2}{12}$ **11.** $21.2 * 5.4$ **12.** $25\overline{)2,050}$

13. $7\overline{)2.45}$ **14.** $\begin{array}{r} 28,931 \\ + \ 16,258 \\ \hline \end{array}$ **15.** $\begin{array}{r} \frac{10}{12} \\ - \ \frac{8}{12} \\ \hline \end{array}$

16. $28\overline{)448}$ **17.** $\frac{1}{4} \times \frac{1}{2}$ **18.** $\begin{array}{r} \frac{10}{16} \\ - \ \frac{8}{16} \\ \hline \end{array}$

19. $\frac{1}{3} \div \frac{2}{3}$ **20.** $\begin{array}{r} 12.054 \\ + \ 96.998 \\ \hline \end{array}$ **21.** $\begin{array}{r} 321.43 \\ - \ 286.56 \\ \hline \end{array}$

22. $\begin{array}{r} \frac{3}{4} \\ * \ \frac{1}{3} \\ \hline \end{array}$ **23.** $\begin{array}{r} \frac{24}{30} \\ + \ \frac{3}{30} \\ \hline \end{array}$ **24.** $\begin{array}{r} 9.9 \\ * \ 81 \\ \hline \end{array}$

25. 129 people came to the school's spaghetti supper. Tickets cost $7.50 per person. How much money did the spaghetti supper make? _____

26. The school paid $224.36 for the food that was served. The people who ran the supper volunteered their time. How much did the supper make, after expenses? _____

27. The student aide made 1,267 photocopies on Monday. On Tuesday, the same aide made 1,209 copies. On Wednesday, he made 382 copies. How many copies did he make in all? _____

Answers to Practice Set 10B

While these problems may be appropriate for fourth grade students, feel free to assign some or all of them to any student who needs practice at this level.

This Practice Set emphasizes addition, subtraction, multiplication, and division of whole numbers, decimals, and fractions. Note the use of two different multiplication symbols (× and ∗) and three different division symbols (/ and ÷ and $\overline{)}$).

Name   Date   Time

Practice Set 10B

Use your favorite strategies to solve the following problems:

1. 428 ∗ 7   2,996   **2.** 739.16 + 58.21 **3.** 5,421 − 4,968   453
            797.37

4. 4,800 / 60   80   **5.** 25,692 + 1,788 **6.** 80.2 × 3.1   248.62
          27,480

7. 6,251.96 − 5,876.21 **8.** 4)$\overline{2,564}$ 641   **9.** 7,183 − 3,926   3,257
     375.75

10. $\frac{3}{11} + \frac{7}{11}$ $\frac{10}{11}$ **11.** 36.1 ∗ 4.2   151.62 **12.** 20)$\overline{3,060}$ 153

13. 8)$\overline{6.56}$ 0.82   **14.** 36,978   **15.** $\frac{8}{11}$
            + 24,438   − $\frac{5}{11}$ $\frac{3}{11}$
            61,416

16. 23)$\overline{322}$ 14   **17.** $\frac{2}{3}$ **18.** $\frac{12}{14}$
         × $\frac{1}{2}$ $\frac{2}{6}$, or $\frac{1}{3}$ − $\frac{1}{14}$ $\frac{11}{14}$

19. $\frac{1}{4} ÷ \frac{3}{4}$ $\frac{4}{12}$, or $\frac{1}{3}$ **20.** 13.263   **21.** 436.21
           + 99.889   − 398.45
          113.152   37.76

22. $\frac{2}{3}$ **23.** $\frac{16}{25}$ **24.** 7.9
   ∗ $\frac{1}{4}$ $\frac{2}{12}$, or $\frac{1}{6}$ + $\frac{5}{25}$ $\frac{21}{25}$ ∗ 39
                 308.1

25. Joe has 129 rocks in his collection. He has a rock polisher that can polish 10 rocks at a time. He has polished 5 batches of rocks. How many rocks are not polished? ___79 rocks___

26. You have 72 cookies and you want to share them equally among you and 17 friends. How many will each person get? ___4 cookies___

27. On Friday Mr. and Mrs. Ruiz drove 165 miles. On Saturday they drove 317 miles. On Sunday they drove 274 miles. How many miles did they drive in all? ___756 miles___

Write your answers on a separate sheet of paper.   **Practice Sets   125**

Practice Set 10B

Use your favorite strategies to solve the following problems:

1. 428 * 7

2. 739.16 + 58.21

3. 5,421 − 4,968

4. 4,800 / 60

5. 25,692 + 1,788

6. 80.2 × 3.1

7. 6,251.96 − 5,876.21

8. 4)$\overline{2,564}$

9. 7,183 − 3,926

10. $\frac{3}{11} + \frac{7}{11}$

11. 36.1 * 4.2

12. 20)$\overline{3,060}$

13. 8)$\overline{6.56}$

14.
$$36,978$$
$$+\ 24,438$$

15.
$$\frac{8}{11}$$
$$-\ \frac{5}{11}$$

16. 23)$\overline{322}$

17.
$$\frac{2}{3}$$
$$\times\ \frac{1}{2}$$

18.
$$\frac{12}{14}$$
$$-\ \frac{1}{14}$$

19. $\frac{1}{4} \div \frac{3}{4}$

20.
$$13.263$$
$$+\ 99.889$$

21.
$$436.21$$
$$-\ 398.45$$

22.
$$\frac{2}{3}$$
$$*\ \frac{1}{4}$$

23.
$$\frac{16}{25}$$
$$+\ \frac{5}{25}$$

24.
$$7.9$$
$$*\ 39$$

25. Joe has 129 rocks in his collection. He has a rock polisher that can polish 10 rocks at a time. He has polished 5 batches of rocks. How many rocks are not polished? _____

26. You have 72 cookies and you want to share them equally among you and 17 friends. How many will each person get? _____

27. On Friday Mr. and Mrs. Ruiz drove 165 miles. On Saturday they drove 317 miles. On Sunday they drove 274 miles. How many miles did they drive in all? _____

Write your answers on a separate sheet of paper.

Answers to Practice Set 11A

While these problems may be appropriate for fifth grade students, feel free to assign some or all of them to any student who needs practice at this level.

This Practice Set emphasizes addition, subtraction, multiplication, and division of whole numbers, decimals, and fractions. Note the use of two different multiplication symbols ($\times$ and $*$) and three different division symbols (/ and $\div$ and $\overline{)}$).

Name   Date   Time

Practice Set 11A

Use your favorite strategies to solve the following problems:

1. 64 * 19   1,216   **2.** 4,800 / 60   80   **3.** 9,307.7 + 4,115.25   13,422.95

4. 620 / 5   124   **5.** 396 / 4   99   **6.** 881.2 + 134.9   1,016.1

7. 1.3 * 5.5   7.15   **8.** 27 * 78   2,106   **9.** 6,981 − 4,367   2,614

10. 10.56 − 9.37   1.19   **11.** 66.2 * 1.4   92.68   **12.** 4,481.35 − 3,842.07   639.28

13.
$$\begin{array}{r} 4,269.00 \\ -\ \ 113.83 \\ \hline 4,115.17 \end{array}$$

14.
$$\begin{array}{r} 72 \\ \times\ 13 \\ \hline 936 \end{array}$$

15. $21\overline{)138.6}$ 6.6

16. 980 / 4   245

17.
$$\begin{array}{r} 5,583.4 \\ -\ \ 496.8 \\ \hline 5,086.6 \end{array}$$

18. $58\overline{)4,872}$ 84

19.
$$\begin{array}{r} 45 \\ \times\ 38 \\ \hline 1,710 \end{array}$$

20.
$$\begin{array}{r} 5.3 \\ \times\ 8.8 \\ \hline 46.64 \end{array}$$

21. $35\overline{)1,225}$ 35

22. 2,068 ÷ 47   44   **23.** 2.76 ÷ 3   0.92   **24.** 429 / 7   61 R2

25. Max can mow 75 square feet of lawn per minute. How many square feet can he mow in an hour?   4,500 square feet

26. To build a tower, Clay used 525 blocks. Each row had 35 blocks. How many rows of blocks were there?   15 rows

27. A scout troop earned $838 in cookie sales. The next year, the troop earned only $615. How much less money did the troop earn the second year? $223 less

Write your answers on a separate sheet of paper.   **Practice Sets 127**

Practice Set 11A

Use your favorite strategies to solve the following problems:

1. 64 * 19

2. 4,800 / 60

3. 9,307.7 + 4,115.25

4. 620 / 5

5. 396 / 4

6. 881.2 + 134.9

7. 1.3 * 5.5

8. 27 * 78

9. 6,981 − 4,367

10. 10.56 − 9.37

11. 66.2 * 1.4

12. 4,481.35 − 3,842.07

13. 4,269.00
    − 113.83

14.   72
    × 13

15. 21)138.6

16. 980 / 4

17.   5,583.4
    − 496.8

18. 58)4,872

19.   45
    × 38

20.   5.3
    × 8.8

21. 35)1,225

22. 2,068 ÷ 47

23. 2.76 ÷ 3

24. 429 / 7

25. Max can mow 75 square feet of lawn per minute. How many square feet can he mow in an hour? _____

26. To build a tower, Clay used 525 blocks. Each row had 35 blocks. How many rows of blocks were there? _____

27. A scout troop earned $838 in cookie sales. The next year, the troop earned only $615. How much less money did the troop earn the second year? _____

Answers to Practice Set 11B

While these problems may be appropriate for fifth grade students, feel free to assign some or all of them to any student who needs practice at this level.

This Practice Set emphasizes addition, subtraction, multiplication, and division of whole numbers, decimals, and fractions. Note the use of two different multiplication symbols ($\times$ and $*$) and three different division symbols (/ and $\div$ and $\overline{)}$).

Name   Date   Time

Practice Set 11B

Use your favorite strategies to solve the following problems:

1. 52 * 37 **1,924**   **2.** 8,400 / 40 **210**   **3.** 5,342.98 + 5,272.01 **10,614.99**

4. 780 / 5 **156**   **5.** 522 / 6 **87**   **6.** 524.13 + 64.32 **588.45**

7. 15.4 * 6.7 **103.18**   **8.** 85 * 97 **8,245**   **9.** 8,567 − 6,399 **2,168**

10. 28.13 − 9.99 **18.14**   **11.** 75.6 * 2.2 **166.32**   **12.** 7,523.81 − 3,449.18 **4,074.63**

13.   85,613.00
− 6,381.85
79,231.15

14.   58
× 85
4,930

15. $3\overline{)1{,}872}$ **624**

16. 780 / 6 **130**

17. 7,456.1 − 621.7
6,834.4

18. $88\overline{)5{,}544}$ **63**

19.   87
× 9.9
861.3

20. 453 * 63 **28,539**

21. $54\overline{)1{,}998}$ **37**

22. 4,002 ÷ 69 **58**   **23.** 3.56 ÷ 4 **0.89**   **24.** 468 / 8 **58 R4**

25. Derek can run one mile in 6 minutes. At this pace, how far can he run in 2 hours? **20 miles in two hours**

27. Randall farms 14 acres of corn. Each acre yields about 275 pounds of corn. About how many pounds of corn will Randall's farm yield?
3,850 pounds of corn

28. Bernie compares prices for the same computer at two different stores. At the first store, the computer costs $680 plus $230 for a printer. At the second store, the computer costs $869.99 and includes a printer. Which computer should Bernie buy and how much money will he save? **The computer from the second store; he will save $40.01**

Write your answers on a separate sheet of paper.

Practice Set 11B

Use your favorite strategies to solve the following problems:

1. 52 * 37

2. 8,400 / 40

3. 5,342.98 + 5,272.01

4. 780 / 5

5. 522 / 6

6. 524.13 + 64.32

7. 15.4 * 6.7

8. 85 * 97

9. 8,567 − 6,399

10. 28.13 − 9.99

11. 75.6 * 2.2

12. 7,523.81 − 3,449.18

13.   85,613.00
     − 6,381.85

14.   58
     × 85

15. 3)1,872

16. 780 / 6

17. 7,456.1 − 621.7

18. 88)5,544

19.   87
    × 9.9

20. 453 * 63

21. 54)1,998

22. 4,002 ÷ 69

23. 3.56 ÷ 4

24. 468 / 8

25. Derek can run one mile in 6 minutes. At this pace, how far can he run in 2 hours? _____

27. Randall farms 14 acres of corn. Each acre yields about 275 pounds of corn. About how many pounds of corn will Randall's farm yield?

_____

28. Bernie compares prices for the same computer at two different stores. At the first store, the computer costs $680 plus $230 for a printer. At the second store, the computer costs $869.99 and includes a printer. Which computer should Bernie buy and how much money will he save?_____

Write your answers on a separate sheet of paper.

Answers to Practice Set 12A

While these problems may be appropriate for fifth grade students, feel free to assign some or all of them to any student who needs practice at this level.

This Practice Set emphasizes addition, subtraction, multiplication, and division of whole numbers, decimals, and fractions. Note the use of two different multiplication symbols ($\times$ and $*$) and two different division symbols ($/$ and $\overline{)}$).

Name   Date   Time

Practice Set 12A

Use your favorite strategies to solve the following problems:

1. $174 * 58$ 10,092

2. $\frac{5}{8} + \frac{2}{8}$ $\frac{7}{8}$

3. $31.1 - 2.14$ 28.96

4. $3,600 / 90$ 40

5. $581 - 339$ 242

6. $1,500 / 50$ 30

7. $39.6 * 22$ 871.2

8. $9,109.52 + 5,662.10$ 14,771.62

9. $823 * 45$ 37,035

10. $715 * 67$ 47,905

11. $630 / 2.5$ 252

12. $\frac{13}{15} - \frac{8}{15}$ $\frac{5}{15}$, or $\frac{1}{3}$

13.
$$\begin{array}{r} 374 \\ \times\ 2.5 \\ \hline 935 \end{array}$$

14. $49\overline{)753}$ 15 R18

15. $36\overline{)2,065}$ 57 R13

16. $589 / 45$ 13 R4

17.
$$\begin{array}{r} 50,135.00 \\ -\ 1,089.16 \\ \hline 49,045.84 \end{array}$$

18.
$$\begin{array}{r} 48,036.163 \\ +\ 1,505.71 \\ \hline 49,541.873 \end{array}$$

19.
$$\begin{array}{r} 235.2 \\ \times\ 78.3 \\ \hline 18,416.16 \end{array}$$

20.
$$\begin{array}{r} 11,898 \\ +\ 4,507 \\ \hline 16,405 \end{array}$$

21.
$$\begin{array}{r} 50,097 \\ -\ 28,459 \\ \hline 21,638 \end{array}$$

22.
$$\begin{array}{r} 7\frac{8}{9} \\ -\ 4\frac{4}{9} \\ \hline \end{array} \ 3\frac{4}{9}$$

23.
$$\begin{array}{r} 52,365.15 \\ +\ 56,325.43 \\ \hline 108,690.58 \end{array}$$

24.
$$\begin{array}{r} 7\frac{5}{6} \\ +\ 5\frac{4}{6} \\ \hline \end{array}$$
$12\frac{9}{6}$, or $13\frac{1}{2}$

25. Carolyn reads 120 words per minute. How many words does she read in 30 minutes?   3,600 words

26. The local movie theater sells about 125 boxes of chocolate-covered raisins each day. About how many boxes does the theater sell in a year?   about 45,625 boxes

27. The Johnsons drove 2,500 miles on the way to their destination and 3,100 miles on the way back. How many miles did the Johnsons drive in all?   5,600 miles

Write your answers on a separate sheet of paper.   **Practice Sets 131**

Practice Set 12A

Use your favorite strategies to solve the following problems:

1. 174 * 58

2. $\frac{5}{8} + \frac{2}{8}$

3. 31.1 − 2.14

4. 3,600 / 90

5. 581 − 339

6. 1,500 / 50

7. 39.6 * 22

8. 9,109.52 + 5,662.10

9. 823 * 45

10. 715 * 67

11. 630 / 2.5

12. $\frac{13}{15} - \frac{8}{15}$

13. $\begin{array}{r} 374 \\ \times\ 2.5 \\ \hline \end{array}$

14. $49\overline{)753}$

15. $36\overline{)2,065}$

16. 589 / 45

17. $\begin{array}{r} 50,135.00 \\ -\ 1,089.16 \\ \hline \end{array}$

18. $\begin{array}{r} 48,036.163 \\ +\ 1,505.71 \\ \hline \end{array}$

19. $\begin{array}{r} 235.2 \\ \times\ 78.3 \\ \hline \end{array}$

20. $\begin{array}{r} 11,898 \\ +\ 4,507 \\ \hline \end{array}$

21. $\begin{array}{r} 50,097 \\ -\ 28,459 \\ \hline \end{array}$

22. $\begin{array}{r} 7\frac{8}{9} \\ -\ 4\frac{4}{9} \\ \hline \end{array}$

23. $\begin{array}{r} 52,365.15 \\ +\ 56,325.43 \\ \hline \end{array}$

24. $\begin{array}{r} 7\frac{5}{6} \\ +\ 5\frac{4}{6} \\ \hline \end{array}$

25. Carolyn reads 120 words per minute. How many words does she read in 30 minutes? _____

26. The local movie theater sells about 125 boxes of chocolate-covered raisins each day. About how many boxes does the theater sell in a year? _____

27. The Johnsons drove 2,500 miles on the way to their destination and 3,100 miles on the way back. How many miles did the Johnsons drive in all? _____

Answers to Practice Set 12B

While these problems may be appropriate for fifth grade students, feel free to assign some or all of them to any student who needs practice at this level.

This Practice Set emphasizes addition, subtraction, multiplication, and division of whole numbers, decimals, and fractions. Note the use of two different multiplication symbols ($\times$ and $*$) and two different division symbols (/ and $\overline{)}$).

Name   Date   Time

Practice Set 12B

Use your favorite strategies to solve the following problems:

1. $275 * 63$ $17,325$ **2.** $\frac{8}{15} + \frac{6}{15}$ $\frac{14}{15}$ **3.** $54.1 - 3.48$ 50.62

4. $6,300 / 70$ 90 **5.** $463 - 296$ 167 **6.** $9,600 / 30$ 320

7. $85.4 * 55$ $4,697$ **8.** $4,653.12 + 527.8$ $5,180.92$ **9.** $547 * 62$ $33,914$

10. $831 * 46$ $38,226$ **11.** $2,975 / 3.5$ 850 **12.** $5\frac{3}{12} - 4\frac{2}{12}$ $1\frac{1}{12}$

13. $\begin{array}{r} 985 \\ \times\ 42.1 \\ \hline 41,468.5 \end{array}$ **14.** $56\overline{)518.00}$ $\overset{9.25}{}$ **15.** $68\overline{)1,392}$ $\overset{20\ R32}{}$

16. $684 / 32$ $21\ R12$ **17.** $\begin{array}{r} 1,284.62 \\ -\ 963.48 \\ \hline 321.14 \end{array}$ **18.** $\begin{array}{r} 82,743.52 \\ +\ \ \ 549.15 \\ \hline 83,292.67 \end{array}$

19. $\begin{array}{r} \$27.45 \\ \times\ \ 15 \\ \hline \$411.75 \end{array}$ **20.** $\begin{array}{r} 648,332 \\ +\ \ 5,348 \\ \hline 653,680 \end{array}$ **21.** $\begin{array}{r} 80,093 \\ -\ 3,799 \\ \hline 76,2974 \end{array}$

22. $\begin{array}{r} 6\frac{8}{18} \\ -\ 6\frac{5}{18} \\ \hline \end{array}$ $\frac{3}{18}$, or $\frac{1}{6}$ **23.** $\begin{array}{r} 45,301.02 \\ +\ \ \ \ 63.99 \\ \hline 45,365.01 \end{array}$ **24.** $\begin{array}{r} 3\frac{7}{12} \\ -\ 2\frac{11}{12} \\ \hline \end{array}$ $\frac{8}{12}$, or $\frac{2}{3}$

25. The circus performs 265 shows per year. They sell 225 sticks of cotton candy at each show. How many sticks of cotton candy do they sell in one year? <u>56,625 sticks of cotton candy</u>

26. Each cotton candy costs $1.50. How much money does the circus take in for cotton candy sales in one year? <u>$89,437.50</u>

27. The Fraser family went on vacation. They drove 5,450 miles in all. Katie drove 2,896 miles. Jeff drove 1,243 miles. Thomas drove the remainder of the way. How many miles did Thomas drive? <u>1,311 miles</u>

Write your answers on a separate sheet of paper.   **Practice Sets   133**

Practice Set 12B

Use your favorite strategies to solve the following problems:

1. 275 * 63

2. $\frac{8}{15} + \frac{6}{15}$

3. 54.1 − 3.48

4. 6,300 / 70

5. 463 − 296

6. 9,600 / 30

7. 85.4 * 55

8. 4,653.12 + 527.8

9. 547 * 62

10. 831 * 46

11. 2,975 / 3.5

12. $5\frac{3}{12} - 4\frac{2}{12}$

13.   985
  × 42.1

14. 56)‾518.00

15. 68)‾1,392

16. 684 / 32

17. 1,284.62
 − 963.48

18. 82,743.52
 + 549.15

19. $27.45
 × 15

20. 648,332
 + 5,348

21. 80,093
 − 3,799

22. $6\frac{8}{18}$
 $-6\frac{5}{18}$

23. 45,301.02
 +   63.99

24. $3\frac{7}{12}$
 $-2\frac{11}{12}$

25. The circus performs 265 shows per year. They sell 225 sticks of cotton candy at each show. How many sticks of cotton candy do they sell in one year? _____

26. Each cotton candy costs $1.50. How much money does the circus take in for cotton candy sales in one year? _____

27. The Fraser family went on vacation. They drove 5,450 miles in all. Katie drove 2,896 miles. Jeff drove 1,243 miles. Thomas drove the remainder of the way. How many miles did Thomas drive? _____

Answers to Practice Set 13A

While these problems may be appropriate for fifth grade students, feel free to assign some or all of them to any student who needs practice at this level.

This Practice Set emphasizes addition, subtraction, multiplication, and division of whole numbers and decimals and fractions. Note the use of two different multiplication symbols ($\times$ and $*$) and three different division symbols (/ and $\div$ and $\overline{)}$).

Name _____ Date _____ Time _____

Practice Set 13A

Use your favorite strategies to solve the following problems:

1. $834 * 12$ $10,008$ **2.** $764.23 + 48.9$ 813.13 **3.** $104.32 * 8.11$ 846.0352

4. $44.33 * 5$ 221.65 **5.** $578 + 2.052$ 580.052 **6.** $3,280 / 4$ 820

7. $\frac{4}{5} - \frac{2}{5}$ $\frac{2}{5}$ **8.** $31,060 * 8$ $248,480$ **9.** $\frac{2}{7} + \frac{3}{7}$ $\frac{5}{7}$

10. $258 / 3$ 86 **11.** $400 * \frac{1}{4}$ 100 **12.** $7,760 \div 16$ 485

13. $\frac{3}{8} + \frac{1}{2}$ $\frac{7}{8}$

14. $\begin{array}{r} 241 \\ \times\ 79 \\ \hline 19,039 \end{array}$

15. $\begin{array}{r} 15.632 \\ +\ 3.446 \\ \hline 19.078 \end{array}$

16. $\frac{1}{2} \times \frac{1}{4}$ $\frac{1}{8}$ **17.** $\frac{1}{2} \times 10$ 5

18. $\begin{array}{r} 506.4 \\ *\ 11.6 \\ \hline 5,874.24 \end{array}$

19. $\begin{array}{r} 0.234 \\ +\ 0.52 \\ \hline 0.754 \end{array}$

20. $3\frac{1}{4} * \frac{1}{4}$ $\frac{13}{16}$

21. $\begin{array}{r} 1.269 \\ -\ 1.178 \\ \hline 0.091 \end{array}$

22. $\frac{5}{8} \times \frac{1}{2}$ $\frac{5}{16}$ **23.** $20\overline{)8.2}$ 0.41 **24.** $5\frac{1}{4} + 2\frac{1}{2}$ $7\frac{3}{4}$

25. Kendra works from 8:00 a.m. until 4:00 p.m. 5 days a week. How many hours does she work each week? _____ 40 hours _____

26. Alex's grandfather was born in 1923. His family had a party for his 75th birthday. In what year was the party? _____ 1998 _____

27. Lincoln had $4.55 to spend on lunch. He bought a sandwich for $1.79. How much did he have left after buying the sandwich? _____ $2.76 _____

Write your answers on a separate sheet of paper.

Practice Set 13A

Use your favorite strategies to solve the following problems:

1. $834 * 12$

2. $764.23 + 48.9$

3. $104.32 * 8.11$

4. $44.33 * 5$

5. $578 + 2.052$

6. $3,280 / 4$

7. $\dfrac{4}{5} - \dfrac{2}{5}$

8. $31,060 * 8$

9. $\dfrac{2}{7} + \dfrac{3}{7}$

10. $258 / 3$

11. $400 * \dfrac{1}{4}$

12. $7,760 \div 16$

13. $\dfrac{3}{8} + \dfrac{1}{2}$

14. $\begin{array}{r} 241 \\ \times\ 79 \\ \hline \end{array}$

15. $\begin{array}{r} 15.632 \\ +\ 3.446 \\ \hline \end{array}$

16. $\dfrac{1}{2} \times \dfrac{1}{4}$

17. $\dfrac{1}{2} \times 10$

18. $\begin{array}{r} 506.4 \\ *\ 11.6 \\ \hline \end{array}$

19. $\begin{array}{r} 0.234 \\ +\ 0.52 \\ \hline \end{array}$

20. $3\dfrac{1}{4} * \dfrac{1}{4}$

21. $\begin{array}{r} 1.269 \\ -\ 1.178 \\ \hline \end{array}$

22. $\dfrac{5}{8} \times \dfrac{1}{2}$

23. $20\overline{)8.2}$

24. $5\dfrac{1}{4} + 2\dfrac{1}{2}$

25. Kendra works from 8:00 a.m. until 4:00 p.m. 5 days a week. How many hours does she work each week? _____

26. Alex's grandfather was born in 1923. His family had a party for his 75th birthday. In what year was the party? _____

27. Lincoln had $4.55 to spend on lunch. He bought a sandwich for $1.79. How much did he have left after buying the sandwich? _____

Answers to Practice Set 13B

While these problems may be appropriate for fifth grade students, feel free to assign some or all of them to any student who needs practice at this level.

This Practice Set emphasizes addition, subtraction, multiplication, and division of whole numbers and decimals. Note the use of two different multiplication symbols (× and ∗) and two different division symbols (/ and ÷).

Name   Date   Time

Practice Set 13B

Use your favorite strategies to solve the following problems:

1. 954 ∗ 15 14,310   **2.** 852.13 + 58.2 910.33   **3.** 402.16 ∗ 7.31 2,939.7896

4. 66.1 ∗ 8.28   **5.** 852 + 7.123 859.123   **6.** 8,240 / 8 1,030
     547.308

7. $\frac{8}{17} - \frac{3}{17}$ $\frac{5}{17}$ **8.** 95,285 ∗ 9 857,565   **9.** $\frac{7}{9} + \frac{1}{9}$ $\frac{8}{9}$

10. 474 / 6 79   **11.** 800 ∗ $\frac{1}{5}$ 160   **12.** 8,874 ÷ 17 522

13. $\frac{8}{11} + \frac{1}{4}$ $\frac{43}{44}$ **14.**   753   **15.**   14.639
                                          × 56   + 5.793
                                       42,168   20.432

16. $\frac{1}{6} \times \frac{3}{7}$ $\frac{3}{42}$ **17.** $\frac{1}{8} \times 16$ 2   **18.**   136.4
                                                                          × 14.6
                                                                       1,991.44

19.   0.463   **20.** $2\frac{1}{3} \ast \frac{1}{3}$ $\frac{7}{9}$ **21.**   1.458
        + 0.279   + 1.999
         0.742   3.457

22. $\frac{3}{7} \times \frac{5}{6}$ **23.** 31.5 ÷ 5 6.3   **24.** $8\frac{1}{4} + 2\frac{1}{2}$ $10\frac{3}{4}$
      $\frac{15}{42}$, or $\frac{5}{14}$

25. Lucy babysits from 4:00 p.m. until 6:00 p.m. every Monday, Wednesday, and Friday. How many hours does she work in 3 weeks? _____ 18 hours _____

26. If she earns $5.50 per hour, how much money does she earn each week? _$33.00 per week_

27. How much money will Lucy earn in one year? _____ $1,716 _____
In three years? _____ $5,148 _____

Write your answers on a separate sheet of paper.   **Practice Sets   137**

Practice Set 13B

Use your favorite strategies to solve the following problems:

1. 954 * 15

2. 852.13 + 58.2

3. 402.16 * 7.31

4. 66.1 * 8.28

5. 852 + 7.123

6. 8,240 / 8

7. $\frac{8}{17} - \frac{3}{17}$

8. 95,285 * 9

9. $\frac{7}{9} + \frac{1}{9}$

10. 474 / 6

11. 800 * $\frac{1}{5}$

12. 8,874 ÷ 17

13. $\frac{8}{11} + \frac{1}{4}$

14.
$$\begin{array}{r} 753 \\ \times\ 56 \\ \hline \end{array}$$

15.
$$\begin{array}{r} 14.639 \\ +\ 5.793 \\ \hline \end{array}$$

16. $\frac{1}{6} \times \frac{3}{7}$

17. $\frac{1}{8} \times 16$

18.
$$\begin{array}{r} 136.4 \\ \times\ 14.6 \\ \hline \end{array}$$

19.
$$\begin{array}{r} 0.463 \\ +\ 0.279 \\ \hline \end{array}$$

20. $2\frac{1}{3} * \frac{1}{3}$

21.
$$\begin{array}{r} 1.458 \\ +\ 1.999 \\ \hline \end{array}$$

22. $\frac{3}{7} \times \frac{5}{6}$

23. 31.5 ÷ 5

24. $8\frac{1}{4} + 2\frac{1}{2}$

25. Lucy babysits from 4:00 p.m. until 6:00 p.m. every Monday, Wednesday, and Friday. How many hours does she work in 3 weeks? _____

26. If she earns $5.50 per hour, how much money does she earn each week? _____

27. How much money will Lucy earn in one year? _____ In three years? _____

Answers to Practice Set 14A

While these problems may be appropriate for fifth grade students, feel free to assign some or all of them to any student who needs practice at this level.

This Practice Set emphasizes addition, subtraction, multiplication, and division of decimals. Note the use of two different multiplication symbols (× and ∗) and three different division symbols (/ and ÷ and ⟌).

Name   Date   Time

Practice Set 14A

Use your favorite strategies to solve the following problems:

1. 9.423 − 6.287 3.136   **2.** 9.024 + 1.832   **3.** 2.49 ∗ 20 49.8
                                        10.856

4. 20⟌6.4 0.32   **5.** 0.246 + 0.28 0.526 **6.** 15.632 − 4.898 10.734

7. 8.631 + 9.878 18.509 **8.** 306.81 × 10.6   **9.** 336.28 ∗ 9.6 3,228.288
                                        3,252.186

10. 9,320.06 − 8,938.09   **11.** 938 / 2.8 335   **12.** 0.688 + 0.39 1.078
              381.97

13. 25⟌13.65 0.546   **14.**   893   **15.** 8⟌6.8 0.85
                                          × 3.8
                                        3,393.4

16.   448   **17.**   48,028.04   **18.**   7.019
           − 77.5   − 1,309.09   + 6.524
           370.5   46,718.95   13.543

19.   22.2   **20.** 26⟌4.55 0.175   **21.** 4.8⟌120 25
           ∗ 8.9
          197.58

22.   0.084   **23.**   39,821.00   **24.**   8.7
           − 0.02   − 6,831.04   × 65
           0.064   32,989.96   565.5

25. Charlotte earns $6.00 per week for mowing two neighbors' lawns. She pays her brother Sam $0.50 to put the grass clippings in the compost heap. After she pays her brother, how much money will she make in 7 weeks? ____$38.50____

26. Cole has $6.25 to buy school supplies. He wants one pack of pens for $1.15, a folder for $2.67, and a pack of paper for $0.99. How much money will he have left over? ____$1.44____

27. Rosita bought four new books for a total of $32.65. What was the average cost per book? ____$8.16____

Write your answers on a separate sheet of paper.   **Practice Sets 139**

Practice Set 14A

Use your favorite strategies to solve the following problems:

1. 9.423 − 6.287

2. 9.024 + 1.832

3. 2.49 * 20

4. 20)6.4

5. 0.246 + 0.28

6. 15.632 − 4.898

7. 8.631 + 9.878

8. 306.81 × 10.6

9. 336.28 * 9.6

10. 9,320.06 − 8,938.09

11. 938 / 2.8

12. 0.688 + 0.39

13. 25)13.65

14.
$$\begin{array}{r} 893 \\ \times\ 3.8 \\ \hline \end{array}$$

15. 8)6.8

16.
$$\begin{array}{r} 448 \\ -\ 77.5 \\ \hline \end{array}$$

17.
$$\begin{array}{r} 48{,}028.04 \\ -\ 1{,}309.09 \\ \hline \end{array}$$

18.
$$\begin{array}{r} 7.019 \\ +\ 6.524 \\ \hline \end{array}$$

19.
$$\begin{array}{r} 22.2 \\ *\ 8.9 \\ \hline \end{array}$$

20. 26)4.55

21. 4.8)120

22.
$$\begin{array}{r} 0.084 \\ -\ 0.02 \\ \hline \end{array}$$

23.
$$\begin{array}{r} 39{,}821.00 \\ -\ 6{,}831.04 \\ \hline \end{array}$$

24.
$$\begin{array}{r} 8.7 \\ \times\ 65 \\ \hline \end{array}$$

25. Charlotte earns $6.00 per week for mowing two neighbors' lawns. She pays her brother Sam $0.50 to put the grass clippings in the compost heap. After she pays her brother, how much money will she make in 7 weeks?

_____

26. Cole has $6.25 to buy school supplies. He wants one pack of pens for $1.15, a folder for $2.67, and a pack of paper for $0.99. How much money will he have left over? _____

27. Rosita bought four new books for a total of $32.65. What was the average cost per book? _____

Write your answers on a separate sheet of paper.

Answers to Practice Set 14B

While these problems may be appropriate for fifth grade students, feel free to assign some or all of them to any student who needs practice at this level.

This Practice Set emphasizes addition, subtraction, multiplication, and division of decimals. Note the use of two different multiplication symbols (× and ∗) and three different division symbols (/ and ÷ and $\overline{)}$).

Name   Date   Time

Practice Set 14B

Use your favorite strategies to solve the following problems:

1. 8.678 − 5.639 3.039   **2.** 545.2 + 120.5   **3.** 7.24 ∗ 60 434.40
                                              665.7

     0.31
4. 30)9.3   **5.** 0.332 + 0.38   **6.** 16.331 − 6.298 10.033
                                              0.712

7. 9.813 + 7.889 17.702 **8.** 241.72 × 11.1   **9.** 421.16 ∗ 9.7 4,085.252
                                        2,683.092

10. 8,930.05 − 6,790.09 **11.** 936 / 2.4 390   **12.** 0.787 + 0.48 1.267
                        2,139.96   0.95
   0.545
13. 22)11.99   **14.**   848   **15.** 6)5.7
                                     × 4.6
                                   3,900.8

16.   329   **17.**   47,054.01   **18.**   8.023
          − 65.5   − 2,109.08   + 6.531
          263.5   44,944.93   14.554

19.   3.53   **20.** 42)5.46 0.13   **21.** 6.2)248 40
          ∗ 9.7
       34.241

22.   0.094   **23.**   36,496.00   **24.**   9.3
          − 0.03   − 7,658.03   × 72
          0.064   28,837.97   669.6

25. Christie bought two pairs of sandals that were $12.99 each. Adam bought two pairs of sandals. His total came to $24.58. Who paid more money overall? _____Christie_____

26. How much did Adam pay per pair of shoes? _____$12.29_____

27. How much more did Christie pay per pair of shoes than Adam? _____$0.70_____

Write your answers on a separate sheet of paper.   **Practice Sets   141**

Practice Set 14B

Use your favorite strategies to solve the following problems:

1. 8.678 − 5.639   **2.** 545.2 + 120.5   **3.** 7.24 ∗ 60

4. 30)9.3   **5.** 0.332 + 0.38   **6.** 16.331 − 6.298

7. 9.813 + 7.889   **8.** 241.72 × 11.1   **9.** 421.16 ∗ 9.7

10. 8,930.05 − 6,790.09 **11.** 936 / 2.4   **12.** 0.787 + 0.48

13. 22)11.99   **14.**   848   **15.** 6)5.7
                                  × 4.6

16.   329   **17.**   47,054.01   **18.**   8.023
         − 65.5   − 2,109.08   + 6.531

19.   3.53   **20.** 42)5.46   **21.** 6.2)248
         ∗ 9.7

22.   0.094   **23.**   36,496.00   **24.**   9.3
         − 0.03   − 7,658.03   × 72

25. Christie bought two pairs of sandals that were $12.99 each. Adam bought
two pairs of sandals. His total came to $24.58. Who paid more money
overall? _____

26. How much did Adam pay per pair of shoes? _____

27. How much more did Christie pay per pair of shoes than Adam?

_____

Answers to Practice Set 15A

While these problems may be appropriate for fifth grade students, feel free to assign some or all of them to any student who needs practice at this level.

This Practice Set emphasizes addition, subtraction, multiplication, and division of fractions. Note the use of two different multiplication symbols ($\times$ and $*$) and three different division symbols (/ and $\div$ and $\overline{)}$).

Name   Date   Time

Practice Set 15A

Use your favorite strategies to solve the following problems:

1. $\frac{5}{8} \times 56$ 35

2. $\frac{4}{8} * \frac{2}{3}$ $\frac{8}{24}$, or $\frac{1}{3}$

3. $\frac{2}{7} + \frac{1}{4}$ $\frac{15}{28}$

4. $\frac{5}{6} - \frac{2}{3}$ $\frac{1}{6}$

5. $\frac{1}{8} \div \frac{5}{8}$ $\frac{8}{40}$, or $\frac{1}{5}$

6. $\frac{11}{36} + \frac{1}{2}$ $\frac{29}{36}$

7. $\frac{4}{5} \times 90$ 72

8. $\frac{8}{9} - \frac{1}{3}$ $\frac{5}{9}$

9. $\frac{2}{3} * \frac{7}{9}$ $\frac{14}{27}$

10. $\frac{3}{6} \div \frac{4}{8}$ $\frac{24}{24}$, or 1

11. $\frac{6}{9} \div \frac{3}{4}$ $\frac{24}{27}$

12. $2\frac{4}{5} + \frac{1}{5}$ $2\frac{5}{5}$, or 3

13. $4\frac{1}{4}$ $\times \frac{2}{9}$ $\frac{34}{36}$, or $\frac{17}{18}$

14. $3\frac{1}{2}$ $+ 1\frac{1}{4}$ $4\frac{3}{4}$

15. $\frac{14}{8}$ $- \frac{6}{8}$ $\frac{8}{8}$, or 1

16. $\frac{4}{5}$ $- \frac{2}{3}$ $\frac{2}{15}$

17. $\frac{8}{12} \div \frac{2}{3}$ $\frac{24}{24}$, or 1

18. $\frac{1}{5}$ $\times \frac{5}{8}$ $\frac{5}{40}$, or $\frac{1}{8}$

19. $\frac{15}{32} \div \frac{5}{8}$ $\frac{120}{160}$, or $\frac{3}{4}$

20. $1\frac{1}{3} \div 2\frac{1}{3}$ $\frac{12}{21}$, or $\frac{4}{7}$

21. $\frac{5}{9}$ $+ \frac{2}{3}$ $1\frac{2}{9}$

22. $\frac{2}{3}$ $\times \frac{1}{3}$ $\frac{2}{9}$

23. $\frac{4}{6}$ $- \frac{3}{8}$ $\frac{7}{24}$

24. $2\frac{1}{3}$ $* \frac{1}{4}$ $\frac{7}{12}$

25. Elliot made 3 of 8 shots in the basketball game. What fraction of the shots did he make? ____ $\frac{3}{8}$ ____

26. What fraction of the shots did he miss in the basketball game? ____ $\frac{5}{8}$ ____

27. If 2 eggs are $\frac{1}{2}$ of the eggs laid by a mother bird, how many eggs did the mother bird lay? ____ 4 eggs ____

Write your answers on a separate sheet of paper.

Practice Set 15A

Use your favorite strategies to solve the following problems:

1. $\frac{5}{8} \times 56$ **2.** $\frac{4}{8} * \frac{2}{3}$ **3.** $\frac{2}{7} + \frac{1}{4}$

4. $\frac{5}{6} - \frac{2}{3}$ **5.** $\frac{1}{8} \div \frac{5}{8}$ **6.** $\frac{11}{36} + \frac{1}{2}$

7. $\frac{4}{5} \times 90$ **8.** $\frac{8}{9} - \frac{1}{3}$ **9.** $\frac{2}{3} * \frac{7}{9}$

10. $\frac{3}{6} \div \frac{4}{8}$ **11.** $\frac{6}{9} \div \frac{3}{4}$ **12.** $2\frac{4}{5} + \frac{1}{5}$

13. $\begin{array}{r} 4\frac{1}{4} \\ \times \frac{2}{9} \\ \hline \end{array}$ **14.** $\begin{array}{r} 3\frac{1}{2} \\ + 1\frac{1}{4} \\ \hline \end{array}$ **15.** $\begin{array}{r} \frac{14}{8} \\ - \frac{6}{8} \\ \hline \end{array}$

16. $\begin{array}{r} \frac{4}{5} \\ - \frac{2}{3} \\ \hline \end{array}$ **17.** $\frac{8}{12} \div \frac{2}{3}$ **18.** $\begin{array}{r} \frac{1}{5} \\ \times \frac{5}{8} \\ \hline \end{array}$

19. $\frac{15}{32} \div \frac{5}{8}$ **20.** $1\frac{1}{3} \div 2\frac{1}{3}$ **21.** $\begin{array}{r} \frac{5}{9} \\ + \frac{2}{3} \\ \hline \end{array}$

22. $\begin{array}{r} \frac{2}{3} \\ \times \frac{1}{3} \\ \hline \end{array}$ **23.** $\begin{array}{r} \frac{4}{6} \\ - \frac{3}{8} \\ \hline \end{array}$ **24.** $\begin{array}{r} 2\frac{1}{3} \\ * \frac{1}{4} \\ \hline \end{array}$

25. Elliot made 3 of 8 shots in the basketball game. What fraction of the shots did he make? _____

26. What fraction of the shots did he miss in the basketball game? _____

27. If 2 eggs are $\frac{1}{2}$ of the eggs laid by a mother bird, how many eggs did the mother bird lay? _____

Write your answers on a separate sheet of paper.

Answers to Practice Set 15B

While these problems may be appropriate for fifth grade students, feel free to assign some or all of them to any student who needs practice at this level.

This Practice Set emphasizes addition, subtraction, multiplication, and division of fractions. Note the use of two different multiplication symbols ($\times$ and $*$) and three different division symbols ($/$ and $\div$ and $\overline{)\ \ }$).

Practice Set 15B

Use your favorite strategies to solve the following problems:

1. $\frac{1}{4} \times 120$ **30**

2. $\frac{6}{8} * \frac{1}{3}$ $\frac{6}{24}$, or $\frac{1}{4}$

3. $\frac{4}{9} + \frac{2}{3}$ $1\frac{1}{9}$, or $\frac{10}{9}$

4. $\frac{6}{7} - \frac{1}{14}$ $\frac{11}{14}$

5. $\frac{1}{6} \div \frac{4}{9}$ $\frac{9}{24}$

6. $\frac{13}{18} + \frac{1}{9}$ $\frac{15}{18}$, or $\frac{5}{6}$

7. $\frac{7}{9} \times 72$ **56**

8. $\frac{17}{20} - \frac{4}{5}$ $\frac{1}{20}$

9. $\frac{3}{4} * \frac{7}{9}$ $\frac{21}{36}$, or $\frac{7}{12}$

10. $\frac{4}{8} \div \frac{5}{10}$ $\frac{40}{40}$, or 1

11. $\frac{7}{9} \div \frac{6}{7}$ $\frac{49}{54}$

12. $2\frac{3}{8} + \frac{5}{8}$ $2\frac{8}{8}$, or 3

13. $\begin{array}{r} 4\frac{1}{4} \\ \times\, \frac{1}{8} \\ \hline \end{array}$ $\frac{17}{32}$

14. $\begin{array}{r} 4\frac{1}{4} \\ +\, 1\frac{1}{2} \\ \hline \end{array}$ $5\frac{3}{4}$

15. $\begin{array}{r} \frac{15}{9} \\ -\, \frac{6}{9} \\ \hline \end{array}$ $\frac{9}{9}$, or 1

16. $\begin{array}{r} \frac{8}{9} \\ -\, \frac{1}{2} \\ \hline \end{array}$ $\frac{7}{18}$

17. $\frac{7}{12} \div \frac{3}{4}$ $\frac{28}{36}$, or $\frac{7}{9}$

18. $\begin{array}{r} \frac{1}{4} \\ \times\, \frac{5}{8} \\ \hline \end{array}$ $\frac{5}{32}$

19. $\frac{5}{40} \div \frac{1}{5}$ $\frac{25}{40}$, or $\frac{5}{8}$

20. $1\frac{1}{4} \div 2\frac{1}{4}$ $\frac{20}{36}$, or $\frac{5}{9}$

21. $\begin{array}{r} \frac{12}{16} \\ +\, \frac{6}{8} \\ \hline \end{array}$ $1\frac{1}{2}$

22. $\begin{array}{r} \frac{2}{8} \\ *\, \frac{1}{2} \\ \hline \end{array}$ $\frac{2}{16}$, or $\frac{1}{8}$

23. $\begin{array}{r} \frac{11}{7} \\ -\, \frac{4}{7} \\ \hline \end{array}$ $\frac{7}{7}$, or 1

24. $\begin{array}{r} 1\frac{1}{4} \\ *\, \frac{2}{3} \\ \hline \end{array}$ $\frac{10}{12}$, or $\frac{5}{6}$

25. If 6 puppies are $\frac{1}{2}$ of a litter, how many puppies are in the entire litter? ____ **12 puppies**

26. Karla made 2 of her 9 goal shots in her soccer game. What fraction of the shots did she make? ____ $\frac{2}{9}$

27. What fraction of the shots did she miss? ____ $\frac{7}{9}$

Write your answers on a separate sheet of paper.   **Practice Sets 145**

Practice Set 15B

Use your favorite strategies to solve the following problems:

1. $\frac{1}{4} \times 120$ **2.** $\frac{6}{8} * \frac{1}{3}$ **3.** $\frac{4}{9} + \frac{2}{3}$

4. $\frac{6}{7} - \frac{1}{14}$ **5.** $\frac{1}{6} \div \frac{4}{9}$ **6.** $\frac{13}{18} + \frac{1}{9}$

7. $\frac{7}{9} \times 72$ **8.** $\frac{17}{20} - \frac{4}{5}$ **9.** $\frac{3}{4} * \frac{7}{9}$

10. $\frac{4}{8} \div \frac{5}{10}$ **11.** $\frac{7}{9} \div \frac{6}{7}$ **12.** $2\frac{3}{8} + \frac{5}{8}$

13. $\quad 4\frac{1}{4}$
$\quad\quad \times \frac{1}{8}$
_____

14. $\quad 4\frac{1}{4}$
$\quad\quad + 1\frac{1}{2}$
_____

15. $\quad \frac{15}{9}$
$\quad\quad - \frac{6}{9}$
_____

16. $\quad \frac{8}{9}$
$\quad\quad - \frac{1}{2}$
_____

17. $\frac{7}{12} \div \frac{3}{4}$

18. $\quad \frac{1}{4}$
$\quad\quad \times \frac{5}{8}$
_____

19. $\frac{5}{40} \div \frac{1}{5}$ **20.** $1\frac{1}{4} \div 2\frac{1}{4}$

21. $\quad \frac{12}{16}$
$\quad\quad + \frac{6}{8}$
_____

22. $\quad \frac{2}{8}$
$\quad\quad * \frac{1}{2}$
_____

23. $\quad \frac{11}{7}$
$\quad\quad - \frac{4}{7}$
_____

24. $\quad 1\frac{1}{4}$
$\quad\quad * \frac{2}{3}$
_____

25. If 6 puppies are $\frac{1}{2}$ of a litter, how many puppies are in the entire litter? _____

26. Karla made 2 of her 9 goal shots in her soccer game. What fraction of the shots did she make? _____

27. What fraction of the shots did she miss? _____

Answers to Practice Set 16A

While these problems may be appropriate for sixth grade students, feel free to assign some or all of them to any student who needs practice at this level.

This Practice Set emphasizes addition, subtraction, multiplication, and division of whole numbers and decimals. Note the use of two different multiplication symbols (× and *) and two different division symbols (/ and $\overline{)}$).

Name   Date   Time

Practice Set 16A

Use your favorite strategies to solve the following problems:

1. 184 * 66   12,144

2. 625 / 25   25

3. 6,091 − 4,438.89   1,652.11

4. 900 / 20   45

5. 750 / 50   15

6. 511 * 37   18,907

7. 1,313.50 − 940.99
      372.51

8. 5,649.4 − 861.87
      4,787.53

9. 7,112.75 + 4,853.71
      11,966.46

10. 620.83 − 349.89
      270.94

11. 1,863 / 34   54 R27

12. 214 * 72   15,408

13.   8,137.2
   − 4,961.4
   3,175.8

14. $\overset{15 \text{ R}10}{86\overline{)1,300}}$

15. $\overset{67 \text{ R}19}{23\overline{)1,560}}$

16.   38,962.8
   + 5,009.7
   43,972.5

17. $\overset{28}{67\overline{)1,876}}$

18.   7,102
   × 30
   213,060

19.   16,238.8
   − 2,459.6
   13,779.2

20.   7,315
   × 59
   431,585

21.   294
   × 23
   6,762

22.   418.02
   × 16.93
  7,077.0786

23.   500.000
   − 123.456
   376.544

24.   13.097
   × 5.681
  74.404057

25. If an airplane travels 525 miles per hour, how far will it fly in 12 hours?   6,300 miles

26. A jet was flying at 33,280 feet and then descended to 17,490 feet. How many feet did the plane descend?   15,790 feet

27. Concession stands in the baseball stadium sell about 22,500 drinks per game. In a season of 164 games, about how many drinks are sold?   about 3,690,000 drinks

Write your answers on a separate sheet of paper.

Practice Set 16A

Use your favorite strategies to solve the following problems:

1. 184 * 66

2. 625 / 25

3. 6,091 − 4,438.89

4. 900 / 20

5. 750 / 50

6. 511 * 37

7. 1,313.50 − 940.99

8. 5,649.4 − 861.87

9. 7,112.75 + 4,853.71

10. 620.83 − 349.89

11. 1,863 / 34

12. 214 * 72

13.   8,137.2
   − 4,961.4

14. 86)‾1,300

15. 23)‾1,560

16.   38,962.8
   + 5,009.7

17. 67)‾1,876

18.   7,102
   ×   30

19.   16,238.8
   − 2,459.6

20.   7,315
   ×   59

21.   294
   × 23

22.   418.02
   × 16.93

23.   500.000
   − 123.456

24.   13.097
   × 5.681

25. If an airplane travels 525 miles per hour, how far will it fly in 12 hours? _____

26. A jet was flying at 33,280 feet and then descended to 17,490 feet. How many feet did the plane descend? _____

27. Concession stands in the baseball stadium sell about 22,500 drinks per game. In a season of 164 games, about how many drinks are sold? _____

Write your answers on a separate sheet of paper.

Answers to Practice Set 16B

While these problems may be appropriate for sixth grade students, feel free to assign some or all of them to any student who needs practice at this level.

This Practice Set emphasizes addition, subtraction, multiplication, and division of whole numbers and decimals. Note the use of two different multiplication symbols (× and *) and two different division symbols (/ and)⎯).

Name   Date   Time

Practice Set 16B

Use your favorite strategies to solve the following problems:

1. 246 * 72 17,712   **2.** 540 / 15 36   **3.** 8,531.52 − 465.894
                                                                8,065.626

4. 3,000 / 75 40   **5.** 1,760 / 20 88   **6.** 741 * 36 26,676

7. 4,556.46 − 978.57   **8.** 8,523.1 − 3,691.52   **9.** 4,582.73 + 27,569.123
        3,577.89   4,831.58   32,151.853

10. 813.76 − 59.99   **11.** 2,648 / 38 69 R26   **12.** 258 * 81 20,898
          753.77

                                       111 R64   280 R20
13.   7,613.280   **14.** 76)8,500   **15.** 28)7,860
        − 4,869.333
        2,743.947

                                       112 R70
16.   83,629.5   **17.** 85)9,590   **18.**   526.4
        + 7,060.76   *   46
        90,690.26   24,214.4

19.   8,239.40   **20.**   2,613   **21.**   5,461
        −   791.36   × 46   × 77
        7,448.04   120,198   420,497

22.   222.85   **23.**   700.01   **24.**   19.73
        × 14.23   − 46.987   × 6.54
      3,171.1555   653.023   129.0342

25. If a cheetah can run 62 miles per hour, how far can it run in 16 hours?
                    992 miles

26. The university enrollment for 1998 was 31,900 students. It was 28,820 in 1999. How much did the enrollment decrease from 1998 to 1999?
       3,080 less students in 1999

27. The average attendance per baseball game for 1999 was 25,860. In a season of 164 games, what was the approximate total attendance for the 1999 season?   4,241,040 people

Write your answers on a separate sheet of paper.   **Practice Sets 149**

Practice Set 16B

Use your favorite strategies to solve the following problems:

1. 246 * 72

2. 540 / 15

3. 8,531.52 − 465.894

4. 3,000 / 75

5. 1,760 / 20

6. 741 * 36

7. 4,556.46 − 978.57

8. 8,523.1 − 3,691.52

9. 4,582.73 + 27,569.123

10. 813.76 − 59.99

11. 2,648 / 38

12. 258 * 81

13.   7,613.280
    − 4,869.333

14. 76)8,500

15. 28)7,860

16.   83,629.5
    + 7,060.76

17. 85)9,590

18.   526.4
    *   46

19.   8,239.40
    −   791.36

20.   2,613
    × 46

21. 5,461
    × 77

22.   222.85
   × 14.23

23.   700.01
   − 46.987

24.   19.73
   × 6.54

25. If a cheetah can run 62 miles per hour, how far can it run in 16 hours?

_____

26. The university enrollment for 1998 was 31,900 students. It was 28,820 in 1999. How much did the enrollment decrease from 1998 to 1999?

_____

27. The average attendance per baseball game for 1999 was 25,860. In a season of 164 games, what was the approximate total attendance for the 1999 season? _____

Answers to Practice Set 17A

While these problems may be appropriate for sixth grade students, feel free to assign some or all of them to any student who needs practice at this level.

This Practice Set emphasizes addition, subtraction, multiplication, and division of whole numbers, decimals, and fractions. Note the use of two different multiplication symbols ($\times$ and $*$) and three different division symbols ($/$ and $\div$ and $\overline{)}$).

Name   Date   Time

Practice Set 17A

Use your favorite strategies to solve the following problems:

1. $8{,}216 * 34$
   279,344

2. $10.890 + 56.31$ **67.2**

3. $3.652 / 4.4$ **0.83**

4. $5{,}263.2 - 774.9$
   4,448.3

5. 41.89×3.25
   136.1425

6. $\frac{2}{6} + \frac{11}{6}$ **$\frac{13}{6}$, or $2\frac{1}{6}$**

7. $9{,}570 * 28$
   267,960

8. $\frac{12}{8} + \frac{5}{8}$ **$\frac{17}{8}$, or $2\frac{1}{8}$**

9. $\frac{4}{9} + \frac{8}{7}$ **$1\frac{37}{63}$**

10. $\frac{7}{9} - \frac{2}{15}$ **$\frac{29}{45}$**

11. $24.32 / 3.8$ **6.4**

12. $\frac{1}{10} - \frac{4}{42}$ **$\frac{1}{210}$**

13. $40\overline{)2{,}290}$ **57 R10**

14. $92\overline{)5{,}620}$ **61 R8**

15. $4\frac{1}{4} * 8\frac{2}{3}$ **$36\frac{5}{6}$**

16. $4\overline{)16.392}$ **4.098**

17. $57\overline{)5{,}260}$ **92 R16**

18. $1{,}006 / 58$ **17 R20**

19. $52\overline{)2{,}500}$ **48 R4**

20. $9\frac{1}{4} * \frac{4}{9}$ **$4\frac{1}{9}$**

21. $\frac{4}{7} \div \frac{6}{11}$ **$1\frac{1}{21}$**

22. $3\frac{2}{7} \div 1\frac{6}{9}$ **$1\frac{34}{35}$**

23. $10{,}080 / 5$ **2,016**

24. $75{,}251 / 3$ **25,083 R2**

25. Melinda's dad's printer can print 3 pages per minute. About how long will it take to print Melinda's 55-page report? **about 18, or 19 minutes**

26. Fairview Heights's population sign changed from 33,094 to 35,118. By how many people did the town's population increase? **by 2,024 people**

27. Trevor's dad drove 4,032 miles in June and 2,897 miles in July. How many total miles did he drive in the 2 months? **6,929 miles**

Write your answers on a separate sheet of paper.   **Practice Sets 151**

Practice Set 17A

Use your favorite strategies to solve the following problems:

1. 8,216 * 34

2. 10.890 + 56.31

3. 3.652 / 4.4

4. 5,263.2 − 774.9

5. 41.89 × 3.25

6. $\frac{2}{6} + \frac{11}{6}$

7. 9,570 * 28

8. $\frac{12}{8} + \frac{5}{8}$

9. $\frac{4}{9} + \frac{8}{7}$

10. $\frac{7}{9} - \frac{2}{15}$

11. 24.32 / 3.8

12. $\frac{1}{10} - \frac{4}{42}$

13. $40\overline{)2,290}$

14. $92\overline{)5,620}$

15. $4\frac{1}{4} * 8\frac{2}{3}$

16. $4\overline{)16.392}$

17. $57\overline{)5,260}$

18. 1,006 / 58

19. $52\overline{)2,500}$

20. $9\frac{1}{4} * \frac{4}{9}$

21. $\frac{4}{7} \div \frac{6}{11}$

22. $3\frac{2}{7} \div 1\frac{6}{9}$

23. 10,080 / 5

24. 75,251 / 3

25. Melinda's dad's printer can print 3 pages per minute. About how long will it take to print Melinda's 55-page report? _____

26. Fairview Heights's population sign changed from 33,094 to 35,118. By how many people did the town's population increase? _____

27. Trevor's dad drove 4,032 miles in June and 2,897 miles in July. How many total miles did he drive in the 2 months? _____

Answers to Practice Set 17B

While these problems may be appropriate for sixth grade students, feel free to assign some or all of them to any student who needs practice at this level.

This Practice Set emphasizes addition, subtraction, multiplication, and division of whole numbers, decimals, and fractions. Note the use of two different multiplication symbols (× and *) and three different division symbols (/ and ÷ and $\overline{)}$).

Name   **Date**   **Time**

Practice Set 17B

Use your favorite strategies to solve the following problems:

1. 5,879 * 46
    270,434

2. 563.12 + 46.55
    609.67

3. 3,312 / 7.2 460

4. 8,319.7 − 528.8
    7,790.9

5. 96.1 × 4.13 396.893

6. $\frac{9}{7} + \frac{3}{7}$ $\frac{12}{7}$, or $1\frac{5}{7}$

7. 4,590 * 34
    156,060

8. $\frac{4}{5} + \frac{3}{5}$ $\frac{7}{5}$, or $1\frac{2}{5}$

9. $\frac{13}{19} + \frac{5}{5}$ $1\frac{13}{19}$

10. $\frac{6}{14} - \frac{1}{14}$ $\frac{5}{14}$

11. 1,121 / 5.9 190

12. $\frac{2}{5} - \frac{1}{10}$ $\frac{3}{10}$

13. $80\overline{)4,570}$ $\overset{57\ R10}{}$

14. $61\overline{)9,696}$ $\overset{158\ R58}{}$

15. $4\frac{1}{8} * 3\frac{1}{9}$ $\frac{924}{72}$, or $12\frac{5}{6}$

16. $18\overline{)6.282}$ $\overset{0.349}{}$

17. $52\overline{)7,920}$ $\overset{152\ R16}{}$

18. 2,004 / 24 83 R12

19. $75\overline{)6,505}$ $\overset{86\ R55}{}$

20. $1\frac{4}{6} * 3\frac{2}{9}$ $5\frac{10}{27}$

21. $2\frac{5}{8} \div \frac{1}{4}$ $10\frac{1}{2}$

22. $7\frac{2}{5} \div 9\frac{1}{10}$ $\frac{74}{91}$

23. 6,736 / 15 449 R1

24. $3.4\overline{)2,723.4}$ $\overset{801}{}$

25. Jack's restaurant sold $35,900.55 during the month of March. If expenses for food and workers were $20,635.89, how much money did the restaurant make in profit for March? _____ $15,264.66 _____

26. Katie drove 3,456 miles in December. Her car gets 32 miles per gallon. How many gallons of gas did Katie use during December? _____ 108 gallons _____

27. Sam can assemble one binder in 4 minutes. How long will it take for him to complete 18 binders? _____ 72 minutes, or _____
    1 hour and 12 minutes

Write your answers on a separate sheet of paper.   **Practice Sets 153**

Practice Set 17B

Use your favorite strategies to solve the following problems:

1. 5,879 $*$ 46

2. 563.12 + 46.55

3. 3,312 / 7.2

4. 8,319.7 − 528.8

5. 96.1 × 4.13

6. $\frac{9}{7} + \frac{3}{7}$

7. 4,590 $*$ 34

8. $\frac{4}{5} + \frac{3}{5}$

9. $\frac{13}{19} + \frac{5}{5}$

10. $\frac{6}{14} - \frac{1}{14}$

11. 1,121 / 5.9

12. $\frac{2}{5} - \frac{1}{10}$

13. $80\overline{)4,570}$

14. $61\overline{)9,696}$

15. $4\frac{1}{8} * 3\frac{1}{9}$

16. $18\overline{)6.282}$

17. $52\overline{)7,920}$

18. 2,004 / 24

19. $75\overline{)6,505}$

20. $1\frac{4}{6} * 3\frac{2}{9}$

21. $2\frac{5}{8} \div \frac{1}{4}$

22. $7\frac{2}{5} \div 9\frac{1}{10}$

23. 6,736 / 15

24. $3.4\overline{)2,723.4}$

25. Jack's restaurant sold $35,900.55 during the month of March. If expenses for food and workers were $20,635.89, how much money did the restaurant make in profit for March? _____

26. Katie drove 3,456 miles in December. Her car gets 32 miles per gallon. How many gallons of gas did Katie use during December?

_____

27. Sam can assemble one binder in 4 minutes. How long will it take for him to complete 18 binders? _____

Write your answers on a separate sheet of paper.

Answers to Practice Set 18A

While these problems may be appropriate for sixth grade students, feel free to assign some or all of them to any student who needs practice at this level.

This Practice Set emphasizes addition, subtraction, multiplication, and division of decimals and fractions. Note the use of two different multiplication symbols ($\times$ and $*$) and three different division symbols ($/$ and $\div$ and $\overline{)}$).

Name   Date   Time

Practice Set 18A

Use your favorite strategies to solve the following problems:

1. $\frac{2}{3} + \frac{1}{6}$ $\frac{5}{6}$

2. $\frac{3}{4} \div \frac{3}{8}$ 2

3. $\frac{7}{9} * \frac{3}{4}$ $\frac{7}{12}$

4. $\frac{8}{5} - \frac{3}{5}$ 1

5. $4\frac{1}{3} * \frac{1}{6}$ $\frac{13}{18}$

6. $853.267 + 0.02$ 853.287

7. $3\frac{1}{2} * 2\frac{2}{3}$ $9\frac{1}{3}$

8. $\frac{7}{9} + \frac{1}{3}$ $1\frac{1}{9}$

9. $3{,}528 / 36$ 98

10. $216 * 32$ $6{,}912$

11. $825 * 432$ $356{,}400$

12. $100.1 * 4.36$ 436.436

13. $\frac{4}{6} \div \frac{6}{7}$ $\frac{7}{9}$

14.
$$\begin{array}{r} 120.000 \\ -\ \ 0.005 \\ \hline 119.995 \end{array}$$

15.
$$\begin{array}{r} 899.02 \\ -\ \ 1.11 \\ \hline 897.91 \end{array}$$

16.
$$\begin{array}{r} 197.83 \\ -120.64 \\ \hline 77.19 \end{array}$$

17.
$$\begin{array}{r} 33.2 \\ \times\ 15 \\ \hline 498 \end{array}$$

18. $4.26\overline{)127.8}$ 30.0

19. $4\overline{)16.392}$ 4.098

20.
$$\begin{array}{r} 355{,}700.39 \\ +\ 24{,}500.63 \\ \hline 380{,}201.02 \end{array}$$

21.
$$\begin{array}{r} 55{,}000 \\ \times\ 0.06 \\ \hline 3{,}300 \end{array}$$

22.
$$\begin{array}{r} 10.345 \\ +\ 0.177 \\ \hline 10.522 \end{array}$$

23. $2 - \frac{3}{4}$ $1\frac{1}{4}$

24. $2\frac{3}{5} - 1\frac{7}{10}$ $\frac{9}{10}$

25. Clara walked 8 blocks to the store. It took her 10 minutes to walk to the store. How long did it take her to walk one block?   **1.25 minutes (or 1 minute 15 seconds)**

26. Marcus drove 665 miles in $9\frac{1}{2}$ hours. Find the average number of miles per hour that Marcus drove.   **70 miles per hour**

27. Sheila bought four books for a total of $50.00. What was the average cost of the books?   **$12.50**

Write your answers on a separate sheet of paper.

Practice Sets 155

Practice Set 18A

Use your favorite strategies to solve the following problems:

1. $\frac{2}{3} + \frac{1}{6}$

2. $\frac{3}{4} \div \frac{3}{8}$

3. $\frac{7}{9} * \frac{3}{4}$

4. $\frac{8}{5} - \frac{3}{5}$

5. $4\frac{1}{3} * \frac{1}{6}$

6. $853.267 + 0.02$

7. $3\frac{1}{2} * 2\frac{2}{3}$

8. $\frac{7}{9} + \frac{1}{3}$

9. $3,528 / 36$

10. $216 * 32$

11. $825 * 432$

12. $100.1 * 4.36$

13. $\frac{4}{6} \div \frac{6}{7}$

14.
$$120.000$$
$$-\ \ 0.005$$

15.
$$899.02$$
$$-\ \ \ 1.11$$

16.
$$197.83$$
$$-\ 120.64$$

17.
$$33.2$$
$$\times\ 15$$

18. $4.26\overline{)127.8}$

19. $4\overline{)16.392}$

20.
$$355,700.39$$
$$+\ 24,500.63$$

21.
$$55,000$$
$$\times\ \ 0.06$$

22.
$$10.345$$
$$+\ 0.177$$

23. $2 - \frac{3}{4}$

24. $2\frac{3}{5} - 1\frac{7}{10}$

25. Clara walked 8 blocks to the store.
It took her 10 minutes to walk to the store.
How long did it take her to walk one block? _____

26. Marcus drove 665 miles in $9\frac{1}{2}$ hours.
Find the average number of
miles per hour that Marcus drove. _____

27. Sheila bought four books for
a total of $50.00. What was
the average cost of the books? _____

Write your answers on a separate sheet of paper.

Answers to Practice Set 18B

While these problems may be appropriate for sixth grade students, feel free to assign some or all of them to any student who needs practice at this level.

This Practice Set emphasizes addition, subtraction, multiplication, and division of decimals and fractions. Note the use of two different multiplication symbols ($\times$ and $*$) and three different division symbols ($/$ and $\div$ and $\overline{)}$).

Name   Date   Time

Practice Set 18B

Use your favorite strategies to solve the following problems:

1. $\frac{5}{8} + \frac{2}{4}$ $1\frac{1}{8}$

2. $3\frac{4}{9} \div 5\frac{1}{8}$ $\frac{248}{369}$

3. $\frac{2}{3} * 1\frac{3}{4}$ $1\frac{1}{6}$

4. $\frac{8}{15} - \frac{7}{15}$ $\frac{1}{15}$

5. $2\frac{3}{7} * \frac{2}{7}$ $\frac{34}{49}$

6. $6{,}138.33 + 0.0056$

                       6,138.3356

7. $8\frac{1}{9} * 2\frac{1}{2}$ $20\frac{5}{18}$

8. $\frac{13}{19} + \frac{5}{5}$ $1\frac{13}{19}$

9. $1{,}876 / 28$ 67

10. $649 * 53.4$

       3,4656.6

11. $951 * 16.7$

       15,881.7

12. $800.2 * 6.52$ 5,217.304

13. $8\frac{6}{7} \div 4\frac{6}{7}$

     $1\frac{28}{34}$, or $1\frac{14}{17}$

14. $\begin{array}{r} 601.001 \\ -\ 0.0606 \\ \hline 600.9404 \end{array}$

15. $161.82 - 99.99$ 61.83

16. $\begin{array}{r} 8{,}793.22 \\ -\ 623.45 \\ \hline 8{,}169.77 \end{array}$

17. $\begin{array}{r} 82.4 \\ \times\ 42 \\ \hline 3{,}460.8 \end{array}$

18. $3.46\overline{)51.90}$ $\overset{15}{}$

19. $7\overline{)258.51}$

     36.93

20. $\begin{array}{r} 444{,}600.29 \\ +\ 6{,}565.369 \\ \hline 451{,}165.659 \end{array}$

21. $\begin{array}{r} 60{,}008 \\ \times\ 0.08 \\ \hline 4{,}800.64 \end{array}$

22. $\begin{array}{r} 20.4896 \\ +\ 2.0006 \\ \hline 22.4902 \end{array}$

23. $6 - \frac{7}{8}$ $5\frac{1}{8}$

24. $8\frac{3}{4} - 6\frac{1}{2}$ $2\frac{1}{4}$

25. Luke walks his neighbor's dog 3.5 miles every day. How many miles does he walk in 30 days? _____105 miles_____

26. He earns $2.25 per day. How much does $15.75 per week; he earn in one week? In one year? __$821.25 in one year_

27. Fran drove $4\frac{4}{10}$ miles from her home to drop her daughter off at soccer practice. Then she drove $2\frac{3}{10}$ miles to the grocery store. She traveled back to pick up her daughter and returned home. How far did Fran travel in all? _____ $13\frac{4}{10}$ miles

Write your answers on a separate sheet of paper.

Practice Sets 157

Practice Set 18B

Use your favorite strategies to solve the following problems:

1. $\frac{5}{8} + \frac{2}{4}$

2. $3\frac{4}{9} \div 5\frac{1}{8}$

3. $\frac{2}{3} * 1\frac{3}{4}$

4. $\frac{8}{15} - \frac{7}{15}$

5. $2\frac{3}{7} * \frac{2}{7}$

6. $6{,}138.33 + 0.0056$

7. $8\frac{1}{9} * 2\frac{1}{2}$

8. $\frac{13}{19} + \frac{5}{5}$

9. $1{,}876 / 28$

10. $649 * 53.4$

11. $951 * 16.7$

12. $800.2 * 6.52$

13. $8\frac{6}{7} \div 4\frac{6}{7}$

14. $\begin{array}{r} 601.001 \\ -\ \ 0.0606 \end{array}$

15. $161.82 - 99.99$

16. $\begin{array}{r} 8{,}793.22 \\ -\ 623.45 \end{array}$

17. $\begin{array}{r} 82.4 \\ \times\ 42 \end{array}$

18. $3.46\overline{)51.90}$

19. $7\overline{)258.51}$

20. $\begin{array}{r} 444{,}600.29 \\ +\ 6{,}565.369 \end{array}$

21. $\begin{array}{r} 60{,}008 \\ \times\ 0.08 \end{array}$

22. $\begin{array}{r} 20.4896 \\ +\ 2.0006 \end{array}$

23. $6 - \frac{7}{8}$

24. $8\frac{3}{4} - 6\frac{1}{2}$

25. Luke walks his neighbor's dog 3.5 miles every day. How many miles does he walk in 30 days? _____

26. He earns $2.25 per day. How much does he earn in one week? In one year? _____

27. Fran drove $4\frac{4}{10}$ miles from her home to drop her daughter off at soccer practice. Then she drove $2\frac{3}{10}$ miles to the grocery store. She traveled back to pick up her daughter and returned home. How far did Fran travel in all? _____

Answers to Practice Set 19A

While these problems may be appropriate for sixth grade students, feel free to assign some or all of them to any student who needs practice at this level.

This Practice Set emphasizes addition, subtraction, multiplication, and division of decimals. Note the use of two different multiplication symbols (× and *) and three different division symbols (/ and ÷ and $\overline{)}$).

Name   Date   Time

Practice Set 19A

Use your favorite strategies to solve the following problems:

1. 3,228.62 − 17.083
3,211.537

2. 856.871 + 0.0023
856.8733

3. 451.2 * 7.8 3,519.36

4. 2.13)31.95 15

5. 98.0065 + 2.9096
100.9161

6. 185.29 − 98.89 86.4

7. 4,628.321 + 16.09
4,644.411

8. 25.6 * 946
24,217.6

9. 608.1 × 7.28 4,426.968

10. 988.01 − 12.11 975.9

11. 129.3 / 8.62 15

12. 3.862 + 481.2 485.062

13. 7.2)16.56   2.3

14.   92.6
* 38
3,518.8

15. 6.28)948.28   151

16.   7,900.56
− 498.9
7,401.66

17.   14.832
− 2.0091
12.8229

18.   698,233.45
+ 8,976.821
707,210.271

19.   101.8
× 5.82
592.476

20. 8)54.8 6.85

21. 18.1)130.32 7.2

22.   110.000
− 0.009
109.991

23.   986.0002
+ 2.13
988.1302

24.   34,821
* 0.09
3,133.89

25. For Thanksgiving, Shirley decided to donate turkeys to a homeless shelter. The total weight of the turkeys she bought was 57.6 pounds. If each turkey averaged 14.4 pounds, how many turkeys did she buy?
_____ 4 turkeys _____

26. If each turkey cost $0.90 per pound, how much did she spend for all of the turkeys? _____ $51.84 _____

27. Mary weighs 79 pounds. On the moon she would weigh only about 0.17 as much. What would Mary's weight be if she were to find herself on the moon? _____ 13.43 pounds _____

Write your answers on a separate sheet of paper.

Practice Sets   159

Practice Set 19A

Use your favorite strategies to solve the following problems:

1. 3,228.62 − 17.083

2. 856.871 + 0.0023

3. 451.2 ∗ 7.8

4. 2.13$\overline{)31.95}$

5. 98.0065 + 2.9096

6. 185.29 − 98.89

7. 4,628.321 + 16.09

8. 25.6 ∗ 946

9. 608.1 × 7.28

10. 988.01 − 12.11

11. 129.3 / 8.62

12. 3.862 + 481.2

13. 7.2$\overline{)16.56}$

14.   92.6
    ∗ 38

15. 6.28$\overline{)948.28}$

16.   7,900.56
  − 498.9

17.   14.832
  − 2.0091

18.   698,233.45
  + 8,976.821

19.   101.8
  × 5.82

20. 8$\overline{)54.8}$

21. 18.1$\overline{)130.32}$

22.   110.000
  −   0.009

23.   986.0002
  +   2.13

24.   34,821
  ∗   0.09

25. For Thanksgiving, Shirley decided to donate turkeys to a homeless shelter. The total weight of the turkeys she bought was 57.6 pounds. If each turkey averaged 14.4 pounds, how many turkeys did she buy?

_____

26. If each turkey cost $0.90 per pound, how much did she spend for all of the turkeys? _____

27. Mary weighs 79 pounds. On the moon she would weigh only about 0.17 as much. What would Mary's weight be if she were to find herself on the moon? _____

Answers to Practice Set 19B

While these problems may be appropriate for sixth grade students, feel free to assign some or all of them to any student who needs practice at this level.

This Practice Set emphasizes addition, subtraction, multiplication, and division of decimals. Note the use of two different multiplication symbols (× and *) and three different division symbols (/ and ÷ and $\overline{)}$).

Name   Date   Time

Practice Set 19B

Use your favorite strategies to solve the following problems:

1. 2,839.58 − 16.092
     2,823.488

2. 6,238.66 + 0.0096
     6,238.6696

3. 628.3 * 8.7 5,466.21

4. 3.4)57.80 17

5. 87.0054 + 14.9098
     101.9152

6. 148.49 − 97.79 50.7

7. 5,821.678 + 17.08
     5,838.758

8. 32.8 * 845 27,716

9. 629.2 × 6.44 4,052.048

10. 994.03 − 8.68
     985.35

11. 134.64 / 7.48 18

12. 2.931 + 622.8 625.731

13. 8.4)26.04 3.1

14.   48.6
   * 97
  4,714.2

15. 7.38)760.14 103

16.   8,300.24
   − 628.8
  7,671.44

17.   16.927
   − 3.0081
  13.9189

18.   575,821.76
   + 7,856.938
  583,678.698

19.   202.6
   × 6.32
  1,280.432

20. 2)49.2 24.6

21. 19.2)157.44 8.2

22.   200.000
   − 0.008
  199.992

23.   799.0003
   + 4.56
  803.5603

24.   54,286
   * 0.08
  4,342.88

25. A large cheeseburger at Henry's Restaurant costs $1.45. If you make one just like it at home the cost is only $0.80. If you made 2 cheeseburgers at home, how much would you save over the two cheeseburgers you would have bought at Henry's restaurant? _____ $1.30 _____

26. Henry's Restaurant took in an average of $315.29 each day last year. How much money overall was taken in that year?
    $115,080.85 _____

27. Betsy has some strips of paper. The strips are 14.23 cm, 7.17 cm, 29.08 cm, and 9.88 cm long. What is the total length of the 4 strips that Betsy has? _____ 60.36 cm _____

Write your answers on a separate sheet of paper.   **Practice Sets 161**

Practice Set 19B

Use your favorite strategies to solve the following problems:

1. 2,839.58 − 16.092   **2.** 6,238.66 + 0.0096   **3.** 628.3 ∗ 8.7

4. 3.4)‾5‾7‾.‾8‾0‾   **5.** 87.0054 + 14.9098   **6.** 148.49 − 97.79

7. 5,821.678 + 17.08   **8.** 32.8 ∗ 845   **9.** 629.2 × 6.44

10. 994.03 − 8.68   **11.** 134.64 / 7.48   **12.** 2.931 + 622.8

13. 8.4)‾2‾6‾.‾0‾4‾   **14.** 48.6 ∗ 97   **15.** 7.38)‾7‾6‾0‾.‾1‾4‾

16. 8,300.24 − 628.8   **17.** 16.927 − 3.0081   **18.** 575,821.76 + 7,856.938

19. 202.6 × 6.32   **20.** 2)‾4‾9‾.‾2‾   **21.** 19.2)‾1‾5‾7‾.‾4‾4‾

22. 200.000 − 0.008   **23.** 799.0003 + 4.56   **24.** 54,286 ∗ 0.08

25. A large cheeseburger at Henry's Restaurant costs $1.45. If you make one just like it at home the cost is only $0.80. If you made 2 cheeseburgers at home, how much would you save over the two cheeseburgers you would have bought at Henry's restaurant? _____

26. Henry's Restaurant took in an average of $315.29 each day last year. How much money overall was taken in that year?

_____

27. Betsy has some strips of paper. The strips are 14.23 cm, 7.17 cm, 29.08 cm, and 9.88 cm long. What is the total length of the 4 strips that Betsy has? _____

Answers to Practice Set 20A

While these problems may be appropriate for sixth grade students, feel free to assign some or all of them to any student who needs practice at this level.

This Practice Set emphasizes addition, subtraction, multiplication, and division of fractions. Note the use of two different multiplication symbols ($\times$ and $*$) and three different division symbols ($/$ and $\div$ and $\overline{)\ \ }$).

Name   Date   Time

Practice Set 20A

Use your favorite strategies to solve the following problems:

1. $\frac{2}{8} \times \frac{1}{3}$ $\frac{1}{12}$

2. $4\frac{1}{8} * 3\frac{3}{4}$ $15\frac{15}{32}$

3. $\frac{9}{4} + \frac{1}{6}$ $2\frac{5}{12}$

4. $\frac{1}{2} - \frac{14}{30}$ $\frac{1}{30}$

5. $\frac{4}{7} \div \frac{6}{11}$ $1\frac{1}{21}$

6. $\frac{13}{19} + \frac{5}{5}$ $1\frac{13}{19}$

7. $\frac{4}{7} * 3\frac{1}{8}$ $1\frac{11}{14}$

8. $\frac{1}{10} - \frac{4}{42}$ $\frac{1}{210}$

9. $3\frac{1}{2} \times 5\frac{1}{3}$ $18\frac{2}{3}$

10. $3\frac{1}{7} \div 1\frac{2}{5}$ $2\frac{12}{49}$

11. $6\frac{4}{8} \div 7\frac{1}{2}$ $\frac{13}{15}$

12. $3\frac{2}{3} + 5\frac{7}{8}$ $9\frac{13}{24}$

13. $\begin{array}{r} 10\frac{3}{5} \\ \times\, 8\frac{7}{5} \\ \hline \end{array}$ $99\frac{16}{25}$

14. $\begin{array}{r} 9\frac{7}{8} \\ +\, 1\frac{9}{12} \\ \hline \end{array}$ $11\frac{5}{8}$

15. $\begin{array}{r} 4\frac{3}{12} \\ -\, \frac{1}{6} \\ \hline \end{array}$ $4\frac{1}{12}$

16. $\begin{array}{r} 3\frac{1}{4} \\ -\, \frac{6}{8} \\ \hline \end{array}$ $2\frac{1}{2}$

17. $7\frac{2}{5} \div 5\frac{1}{10}$ $1\frac{23}{51}$

18. $\begin{array}{r} \frac{46}{12} \\ \times\, \frac{11}{18} \\ \hline \end{array}$ $2\frac{37}{108}$

19. $\frac{2}{3} \div \frac{8}{12}$ 1

20. $2\frac{1}{3} \div 4\frac{7}{12}$

21. $\begin{array}{r} 2\frac{1}{6} \\ +\, \frac{32}{2} \\ \hline \end{array}$ $18\frac{1}{6}$

22. $\begin{array}{r} 4\frac{7}{8} \\ \times\, \frac{2}{7} \\ \hline \end{array}$ $1\frac{11}{28}$

23. $\begin{array}{r} \frac{6}{8} \\ -\, \frac{2}{8} \\ \hline \end{array}$ $\frac{1}{2}$

24. $\begin{array}{r} 33\frac{1}{3} \\ *\, 3 \\ \hline \end{array}$ 100

25. LeAnn paid $\frac{1}{4}$ of the price that Richard paid for 10 pencils. LeAnn paid $2 for the pencils. How much did Richard pay for the pencils? $8.00

26. How much did Richard pay for one pencil? $0.80

27. Pat wants to make a double batch of cookies. If the original recipe calls for $\frac{3}{4}$ cup of sugar, how much sugar should Pat use? $1\frac{1}{2}$ cups

Write your answers on a separate sheet of paper.

Practice Sets 163

Practice Set 20A

Use your favorite strategies to solve the following problems:

1. $\dfrac{2}{8} \times \dfrac{1}{3}$

2. $4\dfrac{1}{8} * 3\dfrac{3}{4}$

3. $\dfrac{9}{4} + \dfrac{1}{6}$

4. $\dfrac{1}{2} - \dfrac{14}{30}$

5. $\dfrac{4}{7} \div \dfrac{6}{11}$

6. $\dfrac{13}{19} + \dfrac{5}{5}$

7. $\dfrac{4}{7} * 3\dfrac{1}{8}$

8. $\dfrac{1}{10} - \dfrac{4}{42}$

9. $3\dfrac{1}{2} \times 5\dfrac{1}{3}$

10. $3\dfrac{1}{7} \div 1\dfrac{2}{5}$

11. $6\dfrac{4}{8} \div 7\dfrac{1}{2}$

12. $3\dfrac{2}{3} + 5\dfrac{7}{8}$

13. $\begin{array}{r} 10\dfrac{3}{5} \\ \times\, 8\dfrac{7}{5} \\ \hline \end{array}$

14. $\begin{array}{r} 9\dfrac{7}{8} \\ +\,1\dfrac{9}{12} \\ \hline \end{array}$

15. $\begin{array}{r} 4\dfrac{3}{12} \\ -\,\dfrac{1}{6} \\ \hline \end{array}$

16. $\begin{array}{r} 3\dfrac{1}{4} \\ -\,\dfrac{6}{8} \\ \hline \end{array}$

17. $7\dfrac{2}{5} \div 5\dfrac{1}{10}$

18. $\begin{array}{r} \dfrac{46}{12} \\ \times\,\dfrac{11}{18} \\ \hline \end{array}$

19. $\dfrac{2}{3} \div \dfrac{8}{12}$

20. $2\dfrac{1}{3} \div 4$

21. $\begin{array}{r} 2\dfrac{1}{6} \\ +\,\dfrac{32}{2} \\ \hline \end{array}$

22. $\begin{array}{r} 4\dfrac{7}{8} \\ \times\,\dfrac{2}{7} \\ \hline \end{array}$

23. $\begin{array}{r} \dfrac{6}{8} \\ -\,\dfrac{2}{8} \\ \hline \end{array}$

24. $\begin{array}{r} 33\dfrac{1}{3} \\ *\ 3 \\ \hline \end{array}$

25. LeAnn paid $\dfrac{1}{4}$ of the price that Richard paid for 10 pencils. LeAnn paid \$2 for the pencils. How much did Richard pay for the pencils?

_____

26. How much did Richard pay for one pencil?

_____

27. Pat wants to make a double batch of cookies.
If the original recipe calls for $\dfrac{3}{4}$ cup of sugar,
how much sugar should Pat use? _____

Answers to Practice Set 20B

While these problems may be appropriate for sixth grade students, feel free to assign some or all of them to any student who needs practice at this level.

This Practice Set emphasizes addition, subtraction, multiplication, and division of fractions. Note the use of two different multiplication symbols ($\times$ and $*$) and three different division symbols ($/$ and $\div$ and $\overline{)}$).

Name   Date   Time

Practice Set 20B

Use your favorite strategies to solve the following problems:

1. $\frac{1}{4} \times \frac{6}{8}$ $\frac{3}{16}$

2. $1\frac{4}{6} * 3\frac{2}{9}$ $5\frac{10}{27}$

3. $\frac{15}{16} + \frac{3}{4}$ $1\frac{11}{16}$

4. $\frac{17}{20} - \frac{4}{5}$ $\frac{1}{20}$

5. $\frac{5}{8} \div \frac{7}{13}$ $1\frac{9}{56}$

6. $\frac{2}{5} + \frac{6}{12}$ $\frac{9}{10}$

7. $\frac{4}{9} * 9\frac{1}{4}$ $4\frac{1}{9}$

8. $\frac{6}{14} - \frac{1}{4}$ $\frac{5}{28}$

9. $6\frac{2}{3} \times 6\frac{2}{3}$ $44\frac{4}{9}$

10. $3\frac{2}{7} \div 1\frac{6}{9}$ $1\frac{34}{35}$

11. $1\frac{1}{10} \div 2\frac{3}{5}$ $\frac{11}{26}$

12. $4\frac{1}{6} + 6\frac{2}{9}$ $10\frac{7}{18}$

13. $\begin{array}{r} 12\frac{1}{3} \\ * \ 8\frac{1}{4} \\ \hline \end{array}$ $101\frac{3}{4}$

14. $\begin{array}{r} 8\frac{3}{4} \\ + \ 2\frac{1}{12} \\ \hline \end{array}$ $10\frac{5}{6}$

15. $\begin{array}{r} 5\frac{3}{4} \\ - \ \frac{1}{2} \\ \hline \end{array}$ $5\frac{1}{4}$

16. $\begin{array}{r} 4\frac{2}{3} \\ - \ \frac{11}{12} \\ \hline \end{array}$ $3\frac{3}{4}$

17. $4\frac{1}{8} \div 2\frac{1}{6}$ $1\frac{47}{52}$

18. $\begin{array}{r} \frac{12}{17} \\ \times \ \frac{21}{12} \\ \hline \end{array}$ $1\frac{12}{51}$

19. $\frac{6}{8} \div \frac{12}{18}$ $1\frac{1}{8}$

20. $4\frac{1}{2} \div 5$ $\frac{9}{10}$

21. $\begin{array}{r} 3\frac{1}{8} \\ + \ \frac{24}{2} \\ \hline \end{array}$ $15\frac{1}{8}$

22. $\begin{array}{r} 3\frac{6}{9} \\ * \ \frac{3}{8} \\ \hline \end{array}$ $1\frac{3}{8}$

23. $\begin{array}{r} \frac{9}{12} \\ - \ \frac{6}{12} \\ \hline \end{array}$ $\frac{1}{4}$

24. $\begin{array}{r} 4\frac{1}{4} \\ * \ \frac{1}{8} \\ \hline \frac{17}{32} \end{array}$

25. If you have read 36 pages, or $\frac{1}{8}$ of the total pages in a book, how many pages are in the entire book? _____ 288 pages

26. How many pages do you have left to read to finish the book? _____ 252 pages

27. A company can produce 800 widgets per day. How many widgets can the factory produce in $3\frac{1}{2}$ days? _____ 2,800 widgets

Write your answers on a separate sheet of paper.

Practice Set 20B

Use your favorite strategies to solve the following problems:

1. $\frac{1}{4} \times \frac{6}{8}$

2. $1\frac{4}{6} * 3\frac{2}{9}$

3. $\frac{15}{16} + \frac{3}{4}$

4. $\frac{17}{20} - \frac{4}{5}$

5. $\frac{5}{8} \div \frac{7}{13}$

6. $\frac{2}{5} + \frac{6}{12}$

7. $\frac{4}{9} * 9\frac{1}{4}$

8. $\frac{6}{14} - \frac{1}{4}$

9. $6\frac{2}{3} \times 6\frac{2}{3}$

10. $3\frac{2}{7} \div 1\frac{6}{9}$

11. $1\frac{1}{10} \div 2\frac{3}{5}$

12. $4\frac{1}{6} + 6\frac{2}{9}$

13. $12\frac{1}{3}$

    $* 8\frac{1}{4}$

14. $8\frac{3}{4}$

    $+ 2\frac{1}{12}$

15. $5\frac{3}{4}$

    $- \frac{1}{2}$

16. $4\frac{2}{3}$

    $- \frac{11}{12}$

17. $4\frac{1}{8} \div 2\frac{1}{6}$

18. $\frac{12}{17}$

    $\times \frac{21}{12}$

19. $\frac{6}{8} \div \frac{12}{18}$

20. $4\frac{1}{2} \div 5$

21. $3\frac{1}{8}$

    $+ \frac{24}{2}$

22. $3\frac{6}{9}$

    $* \frac{3}{8}$

23. $\frac{9}{12}$

    $- \frac{6}{12}$

24. $4\frac{1}{4}$

    $* \frac{1}{8}$

25. If you have read 36 pages, or $\frac{1}{8}$ of the total pages in a book, how many pages are in the entire book? _____

26. How many pages do you have left to read to finish the book? _____

27. A company can produce 800 widgets per day. How many widgets can the factory produce in $3\frac{1}{2}$ days? _____